D0977864

ACCIDENTS IN NORTH AMERICAN MOUNTAINEERING

VOLUME 9 • NUMBER 3 • ISSUE 61
2008

THE AMERICAN ALPINE CLUB
GOLDEN, CO

THE ALPINE CLUB OF CANADA
BANFF, ALBERTA

© 2008 The American Alpine Club

All rights reserved. No part of this publication may be reproduced or transmitted in any form or by any means, electronic or mechanical, including photocopying, recording, or any information and retrieval systems, without permission from the publisher.

ISSN: 0065-082X
ISBN: 978-1-933056-08-1

Manufactured in the United States

Published by:
The American Alpine Club
710 Tenth Street, Suite 100
Golden, CO 80401
www.americanalpineclub.org

Cover Illustrations
Front: Shawangunks—Bonticue Crag. The climb: We call it "Hernia Hang," rated 5.10+ or 5.11, depending on who you ask. [The climber] is on trad lead in this photo. John Okner, photographer.

Back: Near The Dome on Mount Robson. (See Canada accident.) The SOS was stomped out as it appears. It was sent forward by Garth Lemke, Public Safety Warden, ACMG Assistant Ski Guide. Jasper National Park archive photograph.

Printed on recycled paper

CONTENTS

SAFETY ADVISORY COUNCIL 2007

The American Alpine Club
Aram Attarian, John Dill, Mike Gauthier, Chris Harder, Daryl Miller,
Jeff Sheetz, and John E. (Jed) Williamson (Chair)

ACCIDENTS IN
NORTH AMERICAN MOUNTAINEERING
Sixty-First Annual Report of the American Alpine Club

This is the sixty-first issue of *Accidents in North American Mountaineering*. At the time of publication, narratives and data from Canada were not available. However, one report was sent forward by the Public Safety Warden from Mount Robson National Park. Data for the tables will be revised when it is available.

For information on the Alpine Club of Canada, go to:
http://www.alpineclubofcanada.ca/

United States: Please notice that we have changed the name of the American Alpine Club Safety Committee to the Safety Advisory Council. The members of the council have never really met as a committee nor does it have any authority to set policy or take action with matters regarding mountain safety. The individuals have agreed to be "advisory" to the Managing Editor, primarily serving as sources of information and submitting reports. The new title more accurately reflects this role.

In Table III, the category "Other" as an immediate cause of the accident is a high number—28. The list of what these include appears after the tables. Some of them may suggest that we create new line items. A few of the recurring causes include failing to tell guides about a pre-existing medical condition, medical conditions that were unusual (seizure and atrial fibrillation), a medical condition that was self-inflicted (snow blindness), lowering errors (again too many of these), and dislodging rocks. The latter is also scored as "falling rock."

Dislodging rocks comes in a few categories. The most common is when climbers inadvertently dislodge a rock (or rocks) with hands or feet. Mostly this can—and should—be avoided by being careful. Another mechanism is when rocks come loose because climbers are hauling on jammed ropes, which this year accounted for three incidents. An unacceptable form is when a rocks or objects (such as bottles and cans) are purposely thrown down from a summit or ridge. A case such as this that occurred last August will be found under Wyoming.

There are two myths worth mentioning because we hear the wrong sentences being said in conjunction with them all the time.

"As we all know, most accidents occur on the descent, when climbers are fatigued and let their guard down." While the latter part of the statement may be true, the reality is that most *climbing* accidents occur on ascent. If trail hiking were to be considered here, then the whole statement might be true.

"Most accidents occur to inexperienced climbers." The reality is that experienced and moderately experienced climber accidents far outweigh those reported for beginners.

There are some lengthy accounts again this year. They include a few that were submitted by the climbers themselves and a couple that were the result of interviews by diligent rangers.

We always point out that we are not getting reports from some key climbing areas. On the other hand, we are still confident that we are capturing the great majority of accidents that result in fatality or serious injury. As always, we seek help from the climbing corners of the country.

As mentioned in previous issues and throughout this report, there are some web-based resources that often provide good information and accident stories. Here is a short-list of some of those sites:

> http://home.nps.gov/applications/morningreport/
> www.supertopo.com
> http://www.tuckerman.org/
> http://www.mountrainierclimbing.blogspot.com/
> http://www.friendsofyosar.org/

From October 1–3, the Wilderness Risk Management Conference will be held in Jackson Hole, WY, at the Jackson lake Lodge. (Go to http://www.nols.edu/wrmc/committee.shtml for information on the program and registration.)

In addition to the dedicated individuals on the Safety Advisory Council, we are grateful to the following—with apologies for any omissions—for collecting data and for helping with the report: Hank Alacandri, Tom Moyer, Erik Hansen, Leo Paik, Justin Preisendorfer, Robert Speik, Eric White, all individuals who sent in personal stories, and, of course, George Sainsbury.

John E. (Jed) Williamson
Managing Editor
7 River Ridge Road
Hanover, NH 03755
e-mail: jedwmsn@mac.com

CANADA

ROPE AROUND LEG—STUMBLE
British Columbia, Mount Robson National Park, Mount Robson

During the mid-day of July 12th, a team of three were climbing near the top of the Kain Face on Mount Robson. The climbing rope somehow wrapped itself around A.H.'s leg. He stumbled and consequently pulled his groin. The team lowered themselves down the face. The injured climber stayed at the Dome while his two partners descended to Berg Lake where the Robson Ranger Service was notified. The Jasper Warden Service was dispatched early the next morning with a helicopter to pick up the injured person.

Analysis

This incident had potential for much more serious injuries. It stresses the importance of vigilant rope management. Having a rope wrapped around one's leg [while climbing] at any time is not advised. (Source: G. Lemke, Public Safety Warden).

(Editor's Note: This is the only report we have from Canada for this year. The Alpine Club of Canada is recruiting a new editor.)

UNITED STATES

FALL ON ICE—RAPPEL ERROR
Alaska, Denali National Park, Mount Wake
On April 23, Jed Kallen-Brown (23) and Lara Kellogg (38) were climbing the Northeast Ridge of Mount Wake (9,100 feet) in the Ruth Gorge of Denali National Park and Preserve. The pair turned around in the afternoon and began descending the same route. At 1830, while on rappel, Kellogg came off the end of her rope and fatally fell over 1300 feet. Kallen-Brown descended the rest of the route and reached a climbing party in the Ruth Gorge who had a satellite phone. The NPS was notified at 2110 the same day. Kellogg's body was recovered by fixed-wing aircraft on the 24th. She was flown to Talkeetna and transferred to Kehl's Palmer Mortuary.

The following is an excerpt from a statement by Kallen-Brown from an interview at the Talkeetna Ranger Station on the 24th and written documentation he supplied on the 25th: "We began descending and down-climbed to the top of the steep step. At this point she untied before being clipped into the anchor. Not intentional, just happened. I found a good nut, and one 30-meter rappel just barely reached our belay under the overhang. We ate and drank 'bars and water' at this alcove, then fixed one end of the rope to the anchor. The plan was that Lara would rap on the single strand, putting in a couple pieces on the traverse, and I would down-climb. She would either down-climb with me or do a similar rap/down-climb to the top of the first 30-meter step. This had a bulge of good ice at the top that we could V-thread to reach the top of the snow gully.

"I recall pointing out that the single strand 8.5 mm was slippery in her Reverso. We did not put a knot in the end of the rope. She rapped to the traverse, then out of sight. A couple minutes went by, then I heard a scream, 'No!,' that seemed surprised followed by the 'clanking sound' of someone falling, then a thud. As the reality sank in, I tried to calm my nerves. Since she had the whole rack, I couldn't rap if I wanted.

"I packed up the rope and began down-climbing. It was 1830. I came to a Yellow C4 before the traverse, then a Red C3 below it, then a 10-cm screw. Near what must have been the end of the rope, there was a marginal nut. I down-climbed to the top of the step, then made one 30-meter rappel off the ice screw to reach the snow gully. There was an impact mark near a tongue of rock at the bottom of the step. I estimate that she fell 30 meters down 60 to 70 degree ice, then 35 meters of free-fall over the cliff, then about 300 meters of tumbling down the gully. As I down-climbed, I collected tools, screws, and other gear. Her body came to rest near the bottom of the snow cone. I reached it at 1920."

Analysis

Thirteen years, ago almost to the day, two climbers fell and were killed while one was rappelling near the same location on Mount Wake. It should be noted upfront that when rappelling mixed ice, snow, and rock with crampons, the ability to stop and be secure requires added attention and effort. Circumstances of these two accidents are similar, and in both cases, critical accepted rappel procedures were not followed.

A knot was not tied at the end of the rope, which is desirable in many circumstances. Since Kellogg was rappelling in a gully system, there was a greater risk of being hit by falling rocks or ice. If she were to be hit and lose consciousness or control of the rappel, having a knot in the end of the rappel rope could stop the descent.

Kellogg was using the Petzl Reverso (belay/descent control device). Petzl's literature for the Reverso states, "When rappelling on single or half rope, use two strands of rope between 8 and 11mm in diameter, inclusive." She was rappelling on one 8.5mm rope. In a phone call with the US distributor for Petzl, Ranger Roger Robinson asked if a single rope could be used with the Reverso on rappel. He was told that a rope equal to or greater than 10mm could be used, even though they do not provide information on this application. Their literature does indicate that the Reverso can be used with a single rope for belaying, as long as it is at least 10 to 11mm in diameter.

Another safety measure used in these circumstances is to use a sling with an autoblock knot (for webbing) or a prusik knot (for slings) as a back up. She was placing protection, and since she was using an 8.5mm rope that was undersized for her Reverso, the unintentional loss of the rope through it could have occurred while placing the last piece of protection. A back-up system would likely have given her a chance to stop her descent. (There are a number of websites with information on prusik and autoblock set-ups.)

Perhaps it is best to end with a quote from Jed Kallen-Brown: "As I try to piece together the accident, I suspect that she was concentrating on finding gear to belay from and didn't realize how close to the end of the rope she was. Fatigue may have been a contributing factor. I don't know if the slippery rappel system played a part. I do not think she was hit by a rock. I am confident that a knot in the end of the rope would have made the difference. This has certainly caused me to rethink the value judgment that the added security is not worth the hassle of stuck ropes and extra time to tie and untie knots.

"Throughout the day, we were in good spirits, constantly perpetuating one running joke or another. The climbing was enjoyable and the company was unbeatable. Our conversations were never dull. She was always up for a challenge and quite the rope-gun, although she would never admit it. I cherish the time we spent together." (Source: Edited from a report by

Lisa Roderick, Denali National Park, and a report written by Jed Kallen-Brown)

AVALANCHE, CLIMBING UNROPED, PLACED NO PROTECTION
Alaska, Denali National Park, Mount Barrill, Japanese Couloir

On Tuesday evening, May 15th, Andre Callari (33) and Brian Postlethwait (32) set out from their basecamp on the Ruth Glacier to climb the "Japanese Couloir" route on Mount Barrill. Several other parties on the glacier watched them begin their climb. On the 16th the weather was good and there were no sightings of Andre or Brian. On the 17th a team of two ascended half of the Japanese Couloir early in the morning, but chose to retreat due to soft, wet snow conditions. This team reported that Brian and Andre's skis were still at the base of the route. Also on the 17th, a ranger team patrolled from the climbers' basecamp up-glacier around Mount Barrill to the Don Sheldon Mountain House. This entire day was foggy with visibility limited to 300 feet. During this patrol, Ranger Joe Reichert interviewed three groups that had seen the duo begin their climb of Barrill. All of these reporting parties expected to see the team return by late on the 16th or the morning of May 17th, so Reichert alerted the Talkeetna Ranger Station that there was an overdue party on Mount Barrill.

On May 18th, the weather cleared enough in the evening to allow the NPS rescue helicopter to fly into the Ruth Glacier. Rangers John Evans and Reichert flew to investigate at 2100. The remains of the two climbers were quickly located in wet avalanche debris at the base of Mount Barrill's South Face.

On May 19th, the NPS Lama helicopter returned and inserted NPS Mountaineering Rangers Evans and Reichert on the avalanche cone via a step-out operation. One at a time the deceased were flown back to base camp where they were transferred to Talkeetna Air Taxi and flown out to Talkeetna. On this day the ranger team also packed up all of Andre and Brian's basecamp equipment so that it could be returned to the next of kin.

Analysis

The storm that dropped most of the snow involved in this avalanche occurred on May 14th during the day and into that night. On May 15th, the predominant east facing couloir on this route shed most of this new snow in a wet avalanche. Observing that the slide had already occurred, the climbers decided to climb the route. However, where this gully intersects the south ridge, the route traverses on a south and western aspect slope in order to circumvent a gendarme. This is where the fatal avalanche occurred and this slope, being at a higher elevation and different aspect, had not yet stabilized from Monday's storm.

The learning point from this accident is that climbers must re-evaluate snow conditions as terrain and aspect change. Had the climbers chosen to travel roped and place protection, the consequences of the avalanche might have been different. (Source: Edited from a report by Joe Reichert, Ranger)

FALL INTO CREVASSE—UNABLE TO SELF-RESCUE
Alaska, Denali National Park, Mount McKinley, West Buttress

On May 25 about 1900, Val Todd (61) fell into a crevasse at the 7,500-foot level, about 2.5 miles out from basecamp on the Kahiltna Glacier. He dragged his companion, Berlin Nelson (61), until the fall was held by a combination of Nelson, rope drag, and a snow bridge approx 60 feet down. Nelson secured the rope and after determining that Todd was all right, dragged out his sled and pack. Todd was unable to extricate himself due to cold and tiredness, Nelson was also unable to rig a system to haul out the 235-pound Todd, so used their satellite phone to call for assistance.

The initial call went to their service, Talkeetna Air Taxi (TAT). TAT notified basecamp by telephone, and they in turn notified Talkeetna. After further telephone conversation with Nelson, it was decided that a Ranger response was necessary and that the NPS contract Lama would ferry Ranger Evans and two VIP's (Volunteer in Parks) from Base Camp to the scene in order to carry out a rescue.

The Lama arrived at Base Camp at 2115 and picked up Ranger Evans' team to transport them to the scene. The injured team was located fairly easily and by 2125 the Lama was able to land close by (~100m) and the team disembarked and roped up to move to the scene while the Lama returned to basecamp. After assessing the situation by observation and talking to Nelson and Todd, it was decided to rig up a 9:1 haul system in order to extract Todd.

Once Todd was on the surface it could be seen that he had received a blow from his sled causing lacerations around his face, so it was decided that the best thing was to evacuate him and Nelson to basecamp via the Lama for further evaluation. Ranger Evans and the two VIPs were also extracted by the Lama. After further evaluation, it was deemed better for Todd to be flown back to Talkeetna with the Lama and to seek further medical care to clean and suture his wounds.

Analysis

This was a case where the lead climber Nelson had crossed over a hidden snow bridge safely when Todd, with no notice, broke through. The fact that Todd was quite heavily loaded, as well as being a heavy man, led to Nelson not being able to hold the initial fall, so luck was with both of them when Todd landed on the ledge. This arrest might have been helped had they had overhand knots (with loops) in the rope to assist in friction arrest or had they been a rope of three, the recommended number for glacier travel. Once Nelson had anchored the rope securely, one wonders why he was unable to rig up a system to haul Todd up or for Todd to prusik out of the crevasse himself. One wonders whether this was this lack of skill/knowledge or knowing that they had a sat phone and a potential means of rescue from the NPS.

Even if a team has communication with rescue personnel, it is not always possible or practical to get a team to an accident site quickly. Therefore it is incumbent on all teams going into the mountains to be able to perform a self-rescue. This requires knowledge, skill, and a large enough team for the situation. (Source: Edited from a report by John D. Evans, Ranger)

SNOW BLINDNESS—FAILED TO WEAR EYE PROTECTION
Alaska, Denali National Park, Mount McKinley, West Buttress

On June 2, Oure Dalbinco (33) was led by his partner to the medical tent at 14,200 feet. Dalbinco was completely blind in both eyes due to snow blindness. This took longer than normal to heal and due to the severity of the injury, it was deemed safer to fly him off rather than risk him traveling down the glacier. However, due to the prolonged period of unflyable weather, he eventually recovered enough to get down safely with his partner.

Analysis

Even on overcast days, ultra violet rays are strong enough to cause damage to the eyes. It is imperative to wear eye protection in this environment, even when it is overcast. (Source: Edited from a report by John D. Evans, Ranger)

FALL ON SNOW, SPRAIN/STRAIN
Alaska, Denali National Park, Mount McKinley, West Buttress

The "To Zee Top" expedition started their attempt of the West Buttress on June 9 and proceeded on a normal schedule for the climb. After spending several days at the 17,200-foot high camp in poor weather, the team decided to descend on June 28, giving up on a summit attempt. At approximately 1630, while descending the fixed lines around 15,400 feet on the headwall section of the route, Beckie Covill (52) experienced a short fall. The rope system arrested her fall, but she injured her right knee with a twisting motion. Her team members assisted her for a short distance by removing her pack. They continued down slowly. After further evaluation, they called on FRS radio to the Park Service camp at 14,200 feet and formally asked for assistance from the rangers. Rangers Kevin Wright and John Loomis at the 14,200-foot camp received the initial radio call around 1700. At 1750, rangers Wright, Mik Shain, and NPS volunteer Ben Habecker started hiking up to the scene with a Cascade litter, making patient contact at 1857. Covill could not walk and required a litter evacuation back to camp. The rangers splinted the knee and rigged the litter for a vertical evacuation.

At 1940 the patient evacuation started, with Wright and Habecker skiing the litter down the trail and Shain belaying. The initial 300 feet of the evacuation was belayed until the slope angle permitted a safe ski evacuation. At the 14,200-foot camp, the patient was evaluated and determined to have a sprained right knee with possible torn ligaments and cartilage. The patient was released for the night, to be reevaluated the next morning. On the morning of June 29, Covill's knee was still swollen, stiff, and unable to bare weight. The rangers and TZT team members agreed that it would risk further injury to descend the lower glacier on foot. At 0915 the SA-315B Lama helicopter was requested to evacuate the patient to Talkeetna.

Analysis

One of the inherent dangers of mountaineering is the high possibility of small falls with minor injuries. Every mountaineer will experience these injuries given enough time in the mountains. While these injuries are relatively minor in an urban environment, at 15,000 feet in a place like the Alaska Range they can be quite serious. In this situation we were fortunate to have good weather in which to facilitate a relatively easy evacuation.

As a self-supported expedition with experienced members, the TZT expedition probably had sufficient resources to resolve this situation on their own. However, they elected to ask for assistance from the Park Service to make for a safer and more efficient transport to 14,200-foot camp and back to basecamp. Under the circumstances this was probably a prudent decision. In order to transport Beckie Covill back to 14,200-foot camp using only team resources, it may have required leaving some gear behind to retrieve later. It also may have caused further injury to her knee. Likewise the walk to the basecamp landing strip would have required splitting up all the weight between the healthy team members and still may have risked further injury to the patient. Traveling the lower glacier in such poor snow conditions and late in the season would have been extra difficult and hazardous with one team member injured. (Source: Edited from a report by Kevin Wright, Ranger)

ACUTE ABDOMINAL PAIN
Alaska, Denali National Park, Mount McKinley, West Buttress

Alan Arnette (50) registered with the National Park Service as a client with an Alaska Mountaineering School guided expedition (AMS-11) on June 12. Following an uneventful climb to 17,200 feet, Arnette began experiencing difficulties acclimating to the altitude, so his guides decided to escort him back to the 14,200-foot camp to await the return of his expedition. During the descent, Leighan Falley, the AMS guide that was escorting him, radioed the ranger camp that at 1300, her client had experienced an acute onset of abdominal pain accompanied by nausea and vomiting. She declined any assistance at that time but did maintain radio contact throughout the day to keep the ranger staff apprised of their progress. Arnette arrived at the 14,200-foot camp at 2100 and was taken to the rangers for medical examination. He stated that he had experienced a sudden onset of sharp pain, rated 7 out of 10 on a pain scale, throughout the lower quadrants of his abdomen, and accompanied by nausea and vomiting. He had been taking NSAID's and was given a suppository to help alleviate his nausea and vomiting. During his descent he also experienced a bowel movement at the top of the fixed lines at 16,200 feet. This movement was small but the description was indicative of Melina, which was in keeping with a lower gastrointestinal bleed or bowel obstruction. Dr. Jennifer Dow, the NPS physician sponsor, was consulted. She concurred with the probable assessment and recommended an immediate evacuation.

Analysis

Injuries and illnesses are to be expected during a mountaineering expedition and, regrettably, can occur regardless of planning. This was simply a case of bad luck, and it was fortunate that it occurred on descent in a location where his guide was able to assist the client down without much difficulty.

Had this event occurred above 18,200 feet, the evacuation would have been more difficult and hazardous. The patient's guides handled the situation in an exemplary manner and should be commended for recognizing that their client was not doing well physically and taking steps to get him down to lower altitude without outside assistance. (Source: Edited from a report by John Loomis, Ranger)

(Editor's Note: While this is not included as a climbing accident, the narrative is presented for its educational value. There was another abdominal incident that required a helicopter evacuation. In this case, it was suspected that the patient had developed a kidney stone.)

AMS
Alaska, Denali National Park, Mount McKinley, West Buttress

Masamichi Kobayashi (65) was a part of the Tokyo-JAC expedition comprised of four Japanese men. They flew onto the mountain on June 14 and progressed to the 17,200-foot camp in average time. This team shadowed a larger Japanese IARC-JAC team who's leader has been leading expeditions on the mountain for almost 20 years, which included attempting to maintain a weather data collection station above Denali pass.

On June 29, after three days at high camp for acclimatization, the teams departed for the summit and to perform the maintenance on the weather station. Together the group numbered nine climbers. Two members stopped at the weather station (about 18,700 feet), evaluated the damage done the previous winter, cached the tripod remains, and descended to camp. Weather deteriorated slowly during the day, during which the remaining seven climbers gained the summit. (Of interest is that one of Kobayashi's teammates—at age 76—became the oldest man to summit Denali.)

While descending, Kobayashi began to have trouble with his vision. Weather conditions also deteriorated as the winds picked up. The extra assistance that his teammates gave to Kobayashi as well as the weather caused them all to slow down. By 0100 that evening the group had reached Denali Pass, but felt that they could not safely descend to high camp do to the weather and Kobayashi's condition. The seven climbers took shelter next to a rock and shared three bivouac sacs through the coldest part of the night.

On the morning of June 30, the team successfully descended to their high camp and requested that Ranger Tucker Chenoweth evaluate Kobayashi. Upon evaluation, Chenoweth and volunteer EMT Stuart Paterson found rales in the lower lung lobe on the right side and were instructed by sponsoring physician Dr. Dow to continue Nifedipine, administer Albuteral, and begin oxygen therapy.

Due to inclement weather lower on the mountain, the helicopter was unable to evacuate the patient from high camp, so it was decided to lower Kobayashi to the 14,200-foot camp via litter. Chenoweth and his volunteers rigged the anchors and briefed all participants in the details of the operation. At 1836 they began lowering Kobayashi from the 17,200-foot camp using the 3000-foot rescue rope stored there for this purpose. Volunteer Mike Loso was tending the patient for the roped portion of the lowering. At 2017, Loso reached ranger Kevin Wright and his partner Ben Habecker, who relieved Loso and tended Kobayashi on the remaining descent to the 14,200-foot camp, where they arrived at 2154.

Again on July 1st, the weather prevented a helicopter evacuation. Kobayashi was treated with oxygen and in a hyperbaric chamber as ranger John Loomis and his volunteers worked to stabilize him. While his team remained at high camp and helped to put away the gear used in the lowering, Loomis was trying to evaluate Kobayashi to determine if he would regain the strength needed to descend with his team.

Without significant improvement, and because his oxygen saturation dropped into the 60's when removed from supplemental oxygen, it was decided to evacuate Kobayashi by air. At 1039 on July 2, the National Park Service contract Lama Helicopter transported Kobayashi to Talkeetna, where he was transferred to the Aeromed fixed wing aircraft and flown to the hospital in Anchorage. Following an evaluation Kobayashi was released from the hospital on the same day.

Analysis

The National Park Service recommends a time line for ascending the West Buttress that provides most climbers adequate acclimatization. This formula prescribes 10-13 days up to the high camp at 17,200 feet. Kobashi's team moved to high camp on their twelfth day on the mountain, so were well within the average recommended time for the ascent.

Altitude illness can affect anyone, even when they have acclimated properly. Kobayashi had not reported any altitude sickness symptoms prior to their attempt on the summit. This is another case of the unpredictability of altitude related illnesses. This team had the strength and experience to assist their stricken partner and get him back to high camp safely, where they assisted NPS rangers with Kobayashi's evacuation. It is often the case, even with younger climbers, that symptoms do not resolve significantly until the patient returns to low altitude. (Source: Edited from a report by Joe Reichert, Ranger)

HACE
Alaska, Mount McKinley, West Buttress

On June 29 Stefan Jeronin (40), a client of Mountain Trip, collapsed below Denali Pass about 18,000 feet. He was treated on the hill for HACE symptoms and short-roped down to the 17,200-foot camp on the West Buttress, where he was further evaluated by NPS Rangers. It was determined that Jeronin could descend under his own power with short-rope assistance. Jeronin was advised to descend immediately and to be evaluated again by NPS Rangers at the 14,200-foot camp. Showing no additional signs or symptoms, Jeronin descended under his own power with his guide to the 7,200-foot basecamp, where he was flown out by fixed wing to Talkeetna.

Analysis

Summit day on Mount McKinley is a difficult day, both physically and mentally, for everyone, and the extra performance one demands from the body and mind above 17,000 feet are extreme. Jeronin was physically and mentally tired and his body responded accordingly. At 17,800 feet, his condition was treated as altitude illness, and he was escorted to lower altitudes. His diagnosis was inconclusive, but the treatment remains the same at high elevation. Descend, descend, descend. (Source: Edited from a report by Tucker Chenoweth)

(Editor's Note: While not counted as an accident, this case is presented for its valuable lesson.)

SEIZURES—FAILURE TO INFORM GUIDES OF MEDICAL CONDITION
Alaska, Denali National Park, Mount McKinley, West Buttress

A Rainier Mountaineering, Inc. guided party led by Dave Hahn flew to the Kahiltna on June 28 for a climb of Mount McKinley. The nine clients and three guides departed basecamp at 0400 on the June 30. Within a half hour after departing, it began to rain, so the party stopped and set up camp near the bottom of Heart Break Hill on the Kahiltna Glacier. The glacier did not freeze up, but by late morning the weather had improved slightly and several parties were observed traveling back to basecamp. At 1450, RMI departed again traveling for an hour at a time then taking rest breaks. While half way to the 7,800-foot camp and during the second rest break at 1745, client Slayden Douthitt (61) collapsed while taking a sip of water and began exhibiting a series of seizures. Hahn went to his aid and Douthitt slowly came around after three or four minutes. Afterwards, Douthitt felt extremely cold, so he was placed in his sleeping bag within a tent. There were three physicians as clients, one of whom, Dr. Maria Statton, became the primary care giver.

Hahn attempted to reach basecamp with his FRS radio and was picked up by Ranger John Loomis at the 14,200-foot camp at 1755. At 1800, Ranger Joe Reichert at the Talkeetna Ranger Station was notified that Douthitt was unconscious and seizing. Reichert was the IC of another incident, which was in progress.

A medical evacuation with attendants was determined to be essential, so at 1810, Reichert called the Rescue Coordination Center. RCC felt they could launch right away and asked for the coordinates and more information on the patient. At 1815, the patient was reported as AOx4, headache (pain of 7.5 out of10), pulse 120 with respirations of 16. Due to a change in flight crews, the Guard helicopter was delayed at departing and arrived on scene at 2040. Douthitt experienced no further seizures and was transported straight to Providence Hospital in Anchorage.

Analysis

Douthitt was diagnosed by the hospital with intestinal flu and severe dehydration. Douthitt stated that he was "a little achy" in Talkeetna and once he arrived at the basecamp, he felt feverish and was experiencing diarrhea as he began moving on the 30th. Due to the rain, he was wearing his full gortex as they traveled and stated he was "really, really hot" before he collapsed. He was also wet from rain and sweat and mentioned he had difficulty working the zip ventilation on his suit.

If Douthitt had told his guides of his worsening health condition, this evacuation may have been prevented. (Source: Edited from a report by Roger Robinson, Ranger)

(Editor's Note: Clients will often choose not to disclose a medical situation because of their fear of being excluded from the trip and their belief—fantasy—that they will improve once they get started. Experienced climbers are capable of arriving at the last conclusion as well.)

ATRIAL FIBRILLATION
Alaska, Denali National Park, Mount McKinley, West Buttress

Jack Ziegler (50) registered with the National Park Service as a member of a Rainier Mountaineering, Inc., guided expedition, with Greg Collins being the lead guide. The expedition flew onto the mountain via Hudson Air Service and proceeded up on a normal schedule. The expedition ultimately climbed to the 17,200-foot level, arriving there on June 29. Ziegler stated that while at 17,200 feet, he had a feeling of "unwellness." He had experienced a bad headache but that had been relieved by Motrin. He also suffered a bout of nausea that was ameliorated by sitting up and breathing deeply. The lead guide ultimately decided to bring him down to the 14,200-foot camp for evaluation, and then planned on continuing to basecamp. While descending from 17,200 feet, Ziegler stated he felt very exhausted with a lack of energy and SOB (shortness of breath). He felt that this was not normal for him, as he usually felt much better under these conditions because of his level of physical fitness. Upon arrival at 14,200 feet, he immediately went to the Ranger medical camp.

Examination revealed a pulse of 96 with a blood pressure of 80/70 mmHg. Patient had a five-year history of atrial fibrillation, but it had been controlled with a pulmonary vein electrical isolation procedure. Patient was started on 15 LPM oxygen via non-rebreather mask and given 325mg aspirin. This relieved the chest pain, but his blood pressure was still dangerously low. The Lama helicopter was placed on standby for an emergency evacuation and a phone call was made to the patient's cardiologist in New York. A course of medical care was agreed upon and the patient was given a 500cc fluid challenge via an IV bolus of normal saline. This had a salubrious effect, and the patient's vital signs began to stabilize.

However, throughout the rest of the period Ziegler was being treated, his heart rate would not increase to the point necessary to maintain sufficient cardiac output. The decision was made that it would not be in the best interest of the patient if he attempted to walk to basecamp, and so would remain under the care of the NPS. Throughout the entire period Ziegler was at 14,200 feet, he was never able to maintain any physical effort in excess of five minutes. During this period of time, the weather was deteriorating and did not improve sufficiently until July 9, at which time the Lama flew to 14,200 feet and evacuated the patient to the 7,200-foot basecamp. The patient's condition had improved enough so that further evacuation was not required. Following a consultation with the NPS physician sponsor Dr. Jennifer Dow, Ziegler was released following another physical examination by the Park medic at the camp. He flew to Talkeetna on his own with Hudson Air Service. He then went to a cardiologist for consultation.

Analysis

Jack Ziegler did not decide to climb Denali on a whim. Not only was he a physician himself, he had also consulted with his cardiologist prior to the expedition. Atrial fibrillation had not been problematic for the last three years and stress/cardiac tests had proven negative. What occurred was simply a case of bad luck on his part, but it should be noted that this highlights the need for individuals with any sort of cardiac or medical history to be aware that the affliction may suddenly reappear. This is especially true in a harsh environment of high altitude and cold weather. This climber was lucky in that all turned out well. Others on the mountain who have suffered cardiac events have not been as fortunate. (Source: Edited from a report by John Loomis, Ranger)

FALL ON ROCK, PROTECTION PULLED—INADEQUATE PROTECTION, BELAYER IN POOR POSITION
Arizona, Sullivan Canyon, Chino Valley

On March 4, I was climbing a thin, dihedral crack with a bulge about 30 feet up. I had two nuts in below me as I approached the bulge. My belayer was sitting back from the base of the climb about 20 or so feet because the wall was at a lower angle for the first bit of the climb before the crux. The way the rope was running up to me as I climbed over the bulge made the stoppers turn perpendicular to the rock. When I fell, the protection ripped out fairly easily.

Analysis

The two biggest things I took away from my accident are 1) have sufficient gear for the climb and place it correctly; and 2) the climb will always be there. If you aren't feeling strong or confident that day, there are always other climbs. (Source: From a report by the climber, Keo Boulton [18])

FALL ON ROCK, RAPPEL ERROR—NO BACKUP SYSTEM
Arkansas, Buffalo National River Wilderness Area, Hawksbill Crag

On the afternoon of August 25th, a 20-year-old woman was rappelling off a 100-foot bluff near Hawksbill Craig, also known as Whitaker Point, in the Forest Service's Upper Buffalo Wilderness Area. On the way down the bluff, she apparently struck a tree branch, causing her to let her brake hand go. She did not have a belay system in place and fell approximately 30 feet before landing.

Bystanders and members of her group began to assist with her injuries while another bystander hiked out in order to call for help. The Newton County Sheriff's Office received the report and asked the park's SAR team to respond. ALS ambulance, volunteer fire department, and med-evac helicopter personnel arrived first and immediately began hiking toward her location. Due to the steep, rugged and remote terrain, there was no radio communication with the responders hiking to her. NPS and USFS staff began arriving shortly thereafter and a unified command post was set up at the Hawksbill Craig trailhead. By the time NPS and USFS staff hiked to her reported location, she had been stabilized by EMS personnel and carried on a backboard up a break in the bluff line that did not require technical extrication. At the top of the bluff, she was placed in a wheeled litter provided by NPS responders and wheeled approximately three-quarters of a mile to the waiting ambulance. She was then transported to the med-evac helicopter staged in a nearby hayfield and airlifted to Washington Regional Medical Center in Fayetteville, Arkansas.

Her injuries were reported to include two fractured vertebrae and both pelvis and femur fractures. (Source: Lee Buschkowsky, Upper District Range)

Analysis

A belay or an autoblock system is the standard protocol for protecting rappels. (Source: Jed Williamson)

(Editor's Note: A website promoting Arkansas offers the following description of climbing: "The Ozarks of North America offer some of the best rock climbing in mid-America and the clean, uncrowded rock offers a lifetime of rock climbing and bouldering fun. Spend a glorious day in the Arkansas Ozarks learning the skills and techniques of the vertical world. Whether you are a beginner or an extreme rock climber, the 70-80 foot sandstone climbs are perfect for learning or perfecting your skills…"

As the above case illustrates, a better idea would be to learn basic skills before arriving.)

FALL ON SNOW, NO HARD HAT
California, Mount Shasta, Avalanche Gulch

On January 28, a man (44) and his son were attempting to climb the Avalanche Gulch route on Mount Shasta. They were unsuccessful and began descending. Around 1300, the father fell on snow about the 11,500-foot level, sliding 700 feet. A witness to the fall said the climber zipped by him by him at over 30 mph. They descended to him and assessed his injuries. These included a head laceration, broken ribs, and a broken finger. The assisting party helped lower him to Helen Lake (10,400 feet) and awaited assistance from Siskiyou County SAR.

The California Highway Patrol helicopter responded and evacuated the victim at 1700, transporting him to Mercy Medical Center.

Analysis

Below normal snowfall, high winds, and high pressure had left a smooth and hard snow surface. (Source: Eric White, Climbing Ranger/Avalanche Specialist)

STRANDED—BENIGHTED, EXPOSURE— INADEQUATE CLOTHING AND EQUIPMENT, WEATHER, LATE START
California, Yosemite National Park, Royal Arches

My son Sascha (21) and I (54) climbed the Royal Arches (5.7) route in Yosemite Valley on April 10. The weather forecast was sunny and clear for that Tuesday and a chance of rain on Wednesday. We carried a rucksack, 70-meter rope, a large rack of cams, slings, carabiners, etc., helmets, walkie-talkies, three liters of water, some food, a couple of rain parkas, some minimal survival gear, one pair of light gloves, a headlamp, and flashlight. We started the climb at about 8:30 a.m. During most of the morning and early afternoon, I felt confident we could pull this off. We used the walkie-talkies to communicate over the background chatter on the family band frequency. I did all the leading. Around 3 or 4:00 p.m., I became concerned that we weren't moving fast enough to make the North Dome Gully descent in daylight. We completed the final pitch, an exposed, poorly protected 5.4 ramp that was variably wet and covered with pine needles, as the sun was setting. We quickly and sloppily coiled the rope and prepared to hike to the NDG when we noticed that there was quite a bit of water on the granite slab leading into the forest. I didn't want to take any chances, so I decided to rope up for the exposed traverse. Unfortunately, the hastily coiled rope became a rat's nest as I tried to flake it out. This set us back at least a half hour and it was completely unnecessary, since we could have safely done the traverse unroped. We spent the next few hours hiking toward Washington Column to look for the descent route in the moonless dark of night with a headlamp and a flashlight. The satisfaction of completing the climb was quickly replaced with frustration and increasing concern over not finding any resemblance of a trail or a cairn to follow as we headed along the valley rim toward Washington Column. For short distances, never more than a few hundred feet, we were clearly on what looked like a typical climbers' trail heading in the right direction with occasional cairns. It felt like playing "Pin the Tail on the Donkey," only the donkey was several thousand feet away on the other side of a ridge. If you walk in the wrong direction, there is a 2,000-foot drop.

We clumsily made our way up the gently sloping granite slabs over the ridge north of Washington Column. As we descended on the east side of the ridge, we ended up bushwhacking through acres of manzanita. This was exhausting and demoralizing. I grew increasingly concerned that we were depleting our remaining internal resources engaged in a futile exercise. Even if we could find the descent, it would be insane to attempt it on an overcast, moonless night, especially given our level of fatigue. Around 11:00 p.m. we found meager shelter under a nearby boulder for a bivouac. Unbeknownst to us, my wife Ingrid was calling the National Park Service in

Yosemite to notify them that we had not reported back from the climb. As we prepared for our bivouac, I was horrified to realize that we had managed to lose Sascha's rain parka. I struggled to maintain my composure knowing the magnitude of our predicament. We broke open and activated the hand-warmer packages and pretended to sleep. Although I doubt either of us got much sleep, we survived the night reasonably well huddled together to stay warm covered with garbage bags and a space blanket. Cloud cover kept the nighttime low temperature above freezing.

We got up at first light around 6:00 a.m. on Wednesday morning to 80 percent cloud cover and a storm brewing to the east. The visibility was not much better now, but I could see that we were east of Washington Column and a bit too high on the ridge. Apparently we had been following a trail marked with sparse cairns that led somewhere else. I estimated that it would begin snowing within one or two hours, rendering the descent much too dangerous to consider. With less than adequate gear to survive another day of exposure, especially at below freezing temperatures, I began broadcasting using our walkie-talkies. I broadcast for about an hour before someone named Jimmy somewhere in Yosemite Valley responded. I asked Jimmy to contact a ranger and tell him that we were on the rim near Washington Column and didn't think we could survive the impending storm. Less than an hour later I was in radio communication with John Dill of Yosemite Search and Rescue.

Around 8:00 a.m. John Dill went over to Happy Isles to see if he could spot us with his binoculars. At first he couldn't see us, so I waved the space blanket. Over the radio Dill reported that the blanket had appeared in the center of his field-of-view. Now that he had located us, Dill dispatched a three-person team consisting of Keith Lober and two climbing rangers, Rob and Matt, to meet up with us. They began their ascent of the Gully probably around 8:30 a.m. carrying climbing equipment, first aid, fluids, food, and warm clothes.

It began snowing sometime between 7:30 and 8:00 a.m. Initially the snow was light and came at us from the north. We sheltered on the lee side of the wind under pine trees that protected us reasonably well from the snow. This changed about an hour later when the storm increased in intensity and the wind shifted 180 degrees. Cold, wet snow came at us horizontally like we were being sprayed with a fire hose. I sheltered Sascha with the space blanket and garbage bags as best I could as the snow accumulated around us. At one point, Sascha pulled down the space blanket to look at the conditions and he was shocked at what he saw. We were suddenly in winter. Sascha quickly pulled the space blanket back over his head. I radioed YOSAR to inquire about progress. They informed that they were hampered by the storm, but that they would continue to meet with us.

Around 10:00 a.m., Keith Lober reported over the radio that they were near us and that he was sending up flares to see if we could see them. He sent up a total of four flares of which I saw only one as it descended several 100 feet to the east. Keith instructed us to rendezvous with them where Washington Column meets the ridge, the start of the gully descent. Sascha and I started in that direction as the storm raged on. I was becoming increasingly concerned that Sascha's inner core temperature was beginning to drop into hypothermia. Shortly after bushwhacking through acres of manzanita the night before, we passed an ideal bivouac location under a large granite boulder where we could have stayed dry and built a fire. Because I hadn't given up hope of descending at that time, we had passed on this opportunity. In retrospect, that was a mistake.

We scrambled over the snow-covered brush and talus toward the rendezvous location slipping, sliding, and falling like a couple of drunken sailors. As we approached the rendezvous, we came across a boulder that provided enough cover to shelter Sascha. I started calling out to see if they could hear me, while they were using a whistle to try to contact us.

A few minutes later, the storm paused long enough for me to see them about 100 feet away. After making eye contact, I quickly brought Sascha over to them. They immediately assessed Sascha's condition and attended to him. They administered glucose-rich fluids, and provided hot packs and a parka. They also fixed a meal ready to eat (MRE) for him. While the two Rangers attended to Sascha, Keith Lober described how we were to descend. We roped together, with Keith leading and periodically placing pro consisting mainly of slings on trees with an occasional cam device in a crack. I was tied in about 40 to 50 feet behind Keith, then Sascha with Ranger Rob tied in next to him about 50 feet behind me and ranger Matt tied in at the end of the rope. As we descended and Sascha's core temperature recovered, the pain in his extremities was intense and he began screaming. We descended to the valley floor roped together without incident as the storm subsided. We were back down on the valley floor by 2:00 p.m.

Analysis

Do shorter climbs with son to gain experience to prepare for longer routes. Use shorter rope (e.g., 50 meters). Start earlier on long routes. Recognize predicament and find adequate bivy location. Bring survival equipment to build fire and survive snowstorm. Better preparations for descent.

My son and I continue to climb together on shorter routes with relatively straightforward descents. (Source: Victor Madrid)

(Editor's Note: John Dill further advises that one should be careful about relying on cairns, as they do not indicate an official trail in Yosemite. He also suggests seeking advice about tricky descents and bringing a detailed map—and even a photo of the descent route.)

FALLING ROCK—DISLODGED BY CLIMBING PARTNER, POOR POSITION
California, Sierra Nevada, Dunderberg Peak

During the course of the weekend of 27–29 April, I (Peter Francev, 29) met two friends (Jason Hundley, 30, and P.J. Gordon, 29) near Bridgeport, California for an early spring ascent of Dunderberg Peak. Our plan was to climb Dunderberg in preparation for a climb of Mount Shasta's West Face Gully during the following May or June.

Winter conditions in California were warm and dry, so that by the end of April most of the snow on the peaks was melted out, and Dunderberg was no exception. Our plan was to leave the Virginia Lakes trail approximately one mile from the trailhead and climb cross-country over two small benches, so that we could establish a basecamp at Moat Lake. Fortunately, there was a good ground cover of snow atop of the second, higher bench, which also surrounded Moat Lake. Unfortunately, the snow had melted out on the west face of Dunderberg, which, coincidentally, was going to be our route to the summit.

We established basecamp and practiced self-arrest skills on the nearby snow-covered slopes. On the morning of April 29, we awoke at 6:00 a.m. We languished in camp, trying to warm up in the sub-freezing chill and gather the motivation for our climb. At 7:30 a.m., we left camp heading east up the West Face. We were prepared for severe weather carrying extra clothes, and we carried our ice axes and crampons, although neither was needed.

Somewhere near the 11,500-foot mark of Dunderberg's 12,374-foot summit, we came across a narrow chute. After consulting one another, we decided unanimously that Jason would take the lead, I would follow, and P.J. would sweep below. Approximately twenty minutes into the climb up the chute, Jason accidentally dislodged a "basketball-sized" rock that came down, ever so picking up speed. I yelled, "ROCK!" to alert both Jason and P.J. As I watched the rock coming directly at me, I contemplated either moving or turning my back, crouching, and using my backpack to shield myself from the rock. I decided since the rock's fall line was remaining straight that I would quickly move to my left out of its line of descent. I figured that with P.J. being a good 75 to 100 feet below me that he too would be able to get out of harm's way.

I made it about ten feet to the left of the falling rock where at the last second it broke into two almost equal halves. The right half skirted away from my position, but the left half hit me squarely on the inside of the knee. The impact spun me around and I instinctively yelled, which scared both Jason and P.J. At first, I was unsure if I had broken any of the bones in my knee, so I waited a few seconds before I tried to put any pressure on it, let alone try to move it. Before I knew it, both Jason and P.J. were at my side tending to my "needs."

After a few minutes, I was able to put some pressure on the knee. We decided that we should abandon our attempt at Dunderberg and get back to camp as quickly as possible in the event of knee damage. Over the course of the descent, I was able to put some pressure on it, which told me that I was very fortunate to come away with a slight sprain. We made it back to the trailhead and parted our separate ways. The seven-hour drive back to the Los Angeles area, unfortunately, caused the knee to stiffen in place and I was unable to walk without a limp or significant pain for two weeks. I have made a full recovery.

Analysis

As I analyze the course of events that occurred during the climb, I come up with one solution and one lesson learned: First, the accident was merely that... an accident. Even though we took all precautions for this climb, both prior to and during, no one could have foreseen the rock being dislodged. Per the lesson learned: the lack of snow certainly aided in the loosening of the talus, which caused the rock to be dislocated (sic). Even though we were going up a narrow chute and we were spaced out between 75 to 100 feet between each of us, we should have ascended in a horizontal line rather than a vertical line, and if our proximity was still too close, then we should have ascended the chute one-at-a-time. (Source: Edited from a report submitted by Peter Francev.)

(Editor's Note: We respectfully disagree with the notion that "no one could have foreseen the rock being dislodged." This inherent danger requires climbers' constant vigilance, especially under the conditions described. The unfortunate—but never unforeseen—part here is that the falling rock split in half and took a new trajectory.)

PROTECTION PULLED OUT—FALL ON ROCK, INADEQUATE PROTECTION
California, Yosemite National Park, El Capitan

On May 17, Alexander Scola (28) and his partner (23) were on their first climbing trip to the U.S. from their homes in Germany. Scola had been climbing alpine and rock routes for over eleven years and climbed at a high level of difficulty. Most of his experience was in sport and traditional free climbing. He had about one year's experience with aid, however he was competent at placing protection. His partner had been climbing only two years. He had less leading skill and very little aid experience, so Scola was leading most of the pitches. Although they had climbed long alpine routes in Europe, this was their first big wall. This was their second day on the route. They were on schedule and the climb was going well.

Scola had led the King Swing from Boot Flake (pitch 17) and was leading pitch 18, aid-climbing a crack behind a long flake. Like many pitches on El Cap, the crack was of fairly uniform width. Although he carried three of each size of camming device (as recommended in SuperTopo), A.S. felt he should "back-clean" or "leap-frog" his protection, i.e., he would place a cam attached to an etrier/daisy combination, place another while standing in the first etrier, then remove the first cam and place it higher. He planned to occasionally leave a piece in place for protection in case of a fall. This practice left few pieces of protection below him, but he could reuse the same size cams later on the pitch. He had led several pitches on the route this way with no problems but he was left exposed to long falls if a piece failed.

As he started pitch 18, he clipped the rope through a quick-draw on a bolt immediately above the anchor. After climbing about 35 feet using mostly small cams, he left his first piece, a medium-sized, rigid-stem Friend, where the crack began to widen. He clipped a 12-inch sling to the Friend to keep the rope's movement from dislodging the piece. He moved higher on medium Camalots until the Friend was a few feet beneath his feet. At this point, he was an estimated 40-45 feet above the belay.

Just as he removed one Camalot to place it higher, the piece he was weighting with his left foot pulled out and he fell. He had judged the Friend below to be good fall protection when he placed it, but as he fell past it and the rope came tight, he heard a "Pop!" He saw the Friend pull out, and knew he was in for a long fall. The next thing he remembers is waking up dangling ten feet below Eagle Ledge, after a fall of over 100 feet. He was in pain and bleeding from his leg and his face. (It is difficult to know exactly how he was injured. He most likely struck Eagle Ledge before his partner was able to stop the fall with his GriGri, but at the speed he reached, a glancing blow on the wall could have been enough.)

While nearby climbers called for help, his partner rappelled to Eagle Ledge and fashioned a 2:1 mechanical advantage raising system using the haul line. With him pulling from above, Scola was able to use his one good leg to get himself up to Eagle Ledge, where he awaited rescue.

Scola was flown to Memorial Medical Center in Modesto, arriving at the emergency room about four hours after his fall. In addition to a femur fracture, he was diagnosed with compression fractures of three thoracic vertebrae, a minor fracture of the jaw, broken teeth, many bruises, and the loss of about one liter of blood. He is expected to make a full recovery.

Analysis

In retrospect, it was obvious to Scola that he under-protected the pitch. He would normally have left more pieces, especially if free climbing, but it had seemed to him that just standing on aid pieces required fewer protection points. He also may have been overly concerned about running out of specific sizes. He had little experience climbing granite. Other climbers had told him that back-cleaning and leap-frogging were common practices on big wall routes. He had also observed the practice himself many times among other parties climbing near him on the Nose.

Scola's prior experience plus his faith in both of the failed placements underscores the importance of backing yourself up. This isn't a case of a beginner misjudging his protection, nor is this strictly a big wall mistake. It can, and does, happen anywhere. YOSAR has seen several cases of "solid" cam placements failing, even under body weight, with serious injuries and deaths resulting.

Clipping the rope through the directional at the belay was a very smart move. It didn't shorten the fall by much, but it allowed Scola's partner to deal with the force of the catch as an upward pull with his bodyweight helping him instead of yanking him downward and possibly off his stance.

Both climbers get gold stars for wearing their helmets. Scola's helmet was six months old and undamaged prior to the fall. Afterward, the energy-absorbing liner was ruptured in the back and crushed in front. That helmet almost certainly saved his life. (Source: John Dill and Keith Lober, Rangers)

OVERDUE, VARIOUS FALLS ON ROCK, INADEQUATE EQUIPMENT, PARTY SEPARATED, INEXPERIENCE
California, Mount Shasta, Mud Creek Canyon

On June 24 at 1800, the Siskiyou County SAR was notified of a missing 25-year-old female. She had left her partner at 13,600 feet and continued to the summit alone. He waited for her to return but she did not. He became cold enough that he decided to descend and wait for her at Lake Helen. When she still didn't return, he called 911. A California Highway Patrol (CHP) helicopter was used at last light to search for her and was unsuccessful. Due to low light they terminated the air search. USFS Climbing Rangers hiked up from the trailhead in the dark to search for her and other Climbing Rangers searched other likely trailheads on the southeast and east side of the mountain where missing Avalanche Gulch climbers often end up. All Climbing Rangers finished their searches at 0130 on June 25. At 0630, the search continued with the CHP helicopter, USFS Climbing Rangers and Siskiyou County SAR. At 0830 a call was received from a logging camp on the southeast side of the mountain where the missing climber had arrived.

She was interviewed in the hospital. She said that she had reached the summit, made contact with one of the USFS Climbing Rangers and then descended off-route onto the Konwakiton Glacier and below into the steep cliff section in Mud Creek Canyon. She fell several times while descending, receiving multiple bruises and a fractured left arm. She continued down to the lower falls and then climbed out of Mud Creek Canyon and huddled next to a log for the night. The next morning she continued descending until she hit a logging road and later found the logging camp.

Analysis

She had climbed Mount Shasta once before but had no other mountaineering experience. She had no helmet, no ice ax, and no crampons—only "yak trax" on lightweight boots. (Source: Eric White, Climbing Ranger/ Avalanche Specialist)

(Editor's Note: This is one of many cases we see each year in which a hiker finds him or herself in a climbing situation. We do not count these as climbing accidents.)

FALL ON SNOW—FAULTY USE OF CRAMPONS
California, Mount Shasta, Avalanche Gulch

On July 3, a climber fell near The Heart in Avalanche Gulch at 12,500 feet while descending and stuck his crampons into his calf, receiving multiple deep puncture wounds. A USFS Climbing Ranger at Helen Lake made contact with the climber at 1400. The climber refused assistance and descended on his own.

Analysis

An ice ax and crampons are great tools for snow and ice and recommended on all routes on Mount Shasta. However, we see puncture wounds every year due to improper use. One should get some training before using these and continue to practice. (Source: Eric White, Climbing Ranger/Avalanche Specialist)

STRANDED, OFF ROUTE, INADEQUATE EQUIPMENT—LEFT ROPES BEHIND
California, Yosemite Valley National Park, Washington Column

On July 15, two climbers (22 and 20) were attempting to climb the Prow on Washington Column. They decided to retreat from the wall after reaching the top of pitch six. After an attempt to rappel their route, the pair concluded that a retreat down the Prow would be too difficult due to its angled nature. They instead decided to rappel straight down onto what they believed to be the Ten Days After (TDA) route. Neither climber was familiar with the TDA route.

It is believed that the climbers committed to the TDA route at the top of pitch five. The climbers were apparently aware that the TDA route below their position was overhanging. They believed that the descent could be completed by tying their climbing ropes together and rappelling a single strand to a ledge system above the actual base of the wall, since they felt they would not be able to reach intermediary anchors due to the overhanging nature of the wall.

The first climber rappelled with the haul bag. At the very end of the rappel line, he discovered that the ropes were not long enough to reach a stance or an anchor. So he was left hanging at the end of the rope dangling slightly above the desired ledge system, which is still around 100 feet above level ground. He decided to attach his etrier to the bottom of the rope and down-climb to the ledge. He successfully made this transition; however, at some point he lost control of the haul bag and it fell to the base of the wall.

The second climber then descended with a similar technique and made it onto the ledge system where his partner stood. They were still in technical terrain but one of them was not wearing climbing shoes.

They pulled down on the ropes enough that they were able to recover their etrier. At this point they let go of their rope and it predictably recoiled up the wall and out of reach. They were now standing on a small ledge system well above the safety of level ground. They tried to down-climb the remaining 100 feet simultaneously using a 15-foot cordalette tied between them. They were able to get down a short distance, but inevitably it proved to be inadequate as there were not enough usable anchors nor was a 15-foot cordelette long enough to use in the fashion they desired.

At this point they resigned themselves to the realization that they had no other adequate options than to begin yelling for help. A passing climber equipped only with rock shoes came to the their assistance. He solo climbed to the location and guided them down to level ground and out of harm's way.

Analysis

One, it is important to know how to down aid-climb in the event you need to retreat an overhanging or traversing pitch. Two, in general, it is easier to retreat the route you've climbed up or via a route you're familiar with before committing to unknown territory. Finally, leaving your climbing ropes behind while still in vertical terrain is generally a bad idea. (Source: Keith Lober, Ranger and Emergency Services Coordinator)

JUMPED INTO CREVASSE, AND THEN LATER FELL IN CAMP WHILE URINATING
California, Mount Shasta, Hotlum Glacier and in Camp

On August 15, a 28-year-old male climber was hurt when he jumped into a shallow crevasse on the Hotlum Glacier at around 11,400 feet. His crampon caught his pant leg and resulted in a broken tibia.

He was transported by his climbing partners to camp and a Black Hawk came in to evacuate him in the evening. They were unable to hover, so a Chinook was ordered for the following morning.

That night, the injured climber fell when urinating and dislocated his shoulder. His trained team was able to relocate the shoulder and lower him the next morning to an appropriate landing zone at 950 feet. He was then transported to the Weed airport and then taken by vehicle to Mercy Medical Center Mt. Shasta.

Analysis

He was with an experienced trained team who were able to take care of his injuries and transport safely over the glacier and surrounding snowfields. All climbing parties on Mount Shasta should be prepared to handle their own emergencies and know who to call and what to do. (Source: Eric White, Climbing Ranger/Avalanche Specialist)

(Editor's Note: There were very few climbing related incidents on Mount Shasta this year. As usual, however, there were several "lost/missing" cases and a few "party separated" cases. One curious piece of information is that there were 6,200 summit passes sold. This is not uncommon, but the important point is that of this total, not many would be considered climbers.)

FALL ON ROCK, INADEQUATE PROTECTION, OFF ROUTE—LOST TIME, HASTE, DARKNESS
California, Yosemite National Park, Half Dome

On August 19, Robert Kuntz (31) and Ryan Worsham (age unknown) hiked up the slabs approach to the Northwest Face of Half Dome. Their plan was to climb the Regular Route of the Northwest Face (VI 5.9 C1) in a one-day push. After talking to other climbers and reading about the route, they thought this goal was within their ability. They brought limited supplies for the climb, hoping to go light and fast. For their bivy at the base of the route they brought light sleeping bags, fleece jackets, and extra food.

They started climbing at 0630 on Monday, August 20, equipped with a light rack, seven liters of water, and energy food totaling about 700 calories per person. Kuntz wore a long-sleeve wicking top, long pants, wool socks, and shoes. Worsham wore a T-shirt, long pants, shoes, and no socks. They had one beanie, one helmet, and a pair of leather gloves between them. They also brought Kuntz's cellphone, as well as two headlamps for the descent from the summit to their bivy at the base of the route, but left their sleeping bags and jackets at the base.

After the first 11 pitches, they felt they were moving fast enough to finish in daylight. Pitch 12 was Kuntz's lead. He somehow missed the recommended crack and was heading for a 5.9 squeeze variation when he saw what appeared to be an easier passage through the chimney to gain the next belay. This proved to be the wrong way to go and they lost up to an hour and a half reversing the error. Kuntz led the next three pitches of chimneys. After following Pitch 15 on ascenders, Worsham forgot to coil the trailing rope, so it caught in a crack. He had to rappel, free the rope, and re-ascend, thus losing further time. After re-gaining the belay, he led pitch 16.

By the time they reached the start of pitch 17, they realized that they would not complete the route before dark. They decided to sleep on Big Sandy Ledge at the top of 17 and to finish the climb in the morning. While Worsham belayed at a double piton anchor, Kuntz started leading the pitch, anxious to make up for the lost time he felt he had cost them. Kuntz got off route by following a vertical double-crack system before he had traversed far enough to reach Big Sandy. The left-hand crack was wide, requiring a #4

Camalot, which he lacked. The right-hand crack was narrower and shallow in places, but he was forced to use it for protection.

By this time he was improvising direct aid techniques, high-stepping into the protection slings to place the next piece of protection. While standing in the sling attached to the red C3, he placed a gold (#4) Wild Country Zero cam (7) five or six feet higher. He was not confident of the Zero due to the shallowness of the crack and a heavy growth of lichen, which prevented the lobes of the cam from gaining a direct purchase on the rock. However, since the C3 seemed "bomb proof", he thought it was safe enough to try weighting the Zero for aid. He started to pull himself up using the sling attached to the Zero. Suddenly he heard a "ping" and saw the Zero come out of the crack. Since his foot was still in the sling of the C3 cam below, he was pitched off balance and fell upside down and backwards.

At the end of his fall, Kuntz struck hard against a bulge in the wall, first with his lower back and then with his chest and helmet. He never lost consciousness and did not sustain a concussion. Although he had fallen about 50 feet lower than the belay ledge, he was able to climb back up and get into a secure position next to Worsham. Kuntz knew he was probably injured, but he didn't feel any pain immediately.

After a brief discussion about whether or not to continue, they decided that they were done for the day. Once Kuntz stopped moving he started to feel more and more pain radiating around his lower back. He thought he may have broken some ribs and even his spine, but he and Worsham could find no signs of nerve damage, internal bleeding, or other serious injury. When they examined Kuntz's helmet, they found a crack in the back running clear through the foam, but no indentations.

Kuntz's cellphone battery had died during the climb, so there was no way to immediately call for help. They decided they would wait for a party they'd seen at the base to come up the route on Tuesday, or Worsham would descend to them. A third option was to try to climb out. However, as time passed, the pain in Kuntz's back became debilitating and any movement made it worse.

A little after 0300 Tuesday morning, they heard two people chatting on the summit. By shouting and using their headlamps, Kuntz and Worsham were able to communicate their location, the nature of Kuntz's injuries, and their need for a rescue. The party on top contacted the park dispatcher by cellphone.

At 0645, a member of the park's search and rescue (SAR) team contacted them by loudspeaker from the Valley floor. Using arm signals in response to his questions, Kuntz and Worsham were able to describe their situation. By 0945, the SAR team had been placed on the summit by helicopter. They lowered two rescuers and at 1145, they raised Kuntz 600 feet to the top in a litter. He was flown to the Valley, transferred to an air ambulance, and flown to Doctors Medical Center in Modesto. He was diagnosed with torn back muscles and fractures of six spinous and transverse processes of his vertebrae. Luckily there were no life or limb-threatening injuries. He was released within 24 hours, wearing a back brace.

Analysis

Kuntz had seven years of overall climbing experience, including five years of traditional climbing. He had climbed several long alpine free-climbing routes. However, he had not climbed any Yosemite big walls or overnight walls elsewhere. He comfortably led 5.10b traditional and 5.10c sport climbs, and had led aid climbs up to C-2. Worsham had ten years of climbing experience. He also had limited aid-climbing experience and had not completed any Yosemite-style big walls.

The immediate cause of Kuntz's long fall and the resulting injury is the fact that the rope was not clipped through the Camalot C3. Otherwise, the fall probably would have been short and of little consequence. Kuntz feels that a significant contributing cause was haste. After the team fell behind on pitch 12, he felt rushed to make up the lost time or to at least reach Big Sandy Ledge for the night. He fell victim to "tunnel vision," i.e., he became less aware of his options. In Kuntz's opinion, several other factors affected their situation.

• Seven liters of water was one or two liters too much. It added unnecessary weight, slowing them down.

• A #4 Camalot would have been useful, especially in chimneys.

• Leaving their warm fleece jackets and emergency food at the base led to a very cold night.

• Kuntz's foam helmet provided significant insulation against the cold that night.

• They should have brought *two* helmets. In addition to the usual reasons, rocks launched from the summit by tourists and a haul bag dropped by climbers above narrowly missed them.

(Source: Contributions by Jesse McGahey and John Dill, Ranger)

FALL ON ROCK—BELAY FAILURE, NO STOPPER KNOT, MISSED CLUES, INATTENTION, NO HARD HAT
California, Yosemite Valley National Park, Church Bowl

On October 12, Adam (31), Jason (57) and his son Colby (20) were climbing one-pitch routes at the Church Bowl climbing area using a 70m (230-foot) rope. Adam consulted the SuperTopo guide for route data and they picked out climbs as they went along.

Adam belayed from the ground as Colby led Church Bowl Lieback (5.8). Colby built the top anchor, then Adam lowered him. As Colby reached the ground, Adam recalls, "I looked down at the belay rope and said, 'Oh, that's close! The end's right there.' It was hard to tell because of rope stretch, but we had only a few feet left—really close. However, the end was tied to the rope bag, so it wouldn't have gone through my GriGri."

After Adam and Jason had each top-roped Lieback and been lowered, they pulled the rope, leaving the anchor in place at the top. Then Colby led Pole Position (5.10), a few feet to the right of Lieback. Instead of climbing to the top of Pole Position, he finished the crux, then set up the top-rope by clipping the rope through a directional bolt on Pole Position and using the original Lieback anchor a few feet to the left. Because of the directional, the top-rope on Pole Position required more rope than Lieback had but less than if Colby had climbed the full 130 feet of Pole Position.

Adam lowered Colby through the directional. "We had less rope left when Colby reached the ground than on Lieback—just enough to control the GriGri as the next climber started up," he says. Adam climbed Pole Position next as Jason belayed, then Jason climbed as Colby belayed.

Meanwhile, they had noticed Revival, another 130-foot, 5.10 pitch about 20 feet right of Pole Position. Lunchtime wasn't far off, so rather than lead Revival, they decided that Jason would move the top-rope over when he climbed Pole Position.

After finishing Pole Position, Jason took the rope and the rigging from the Lieback anchor and scrambled several feet right and about ten feet higher to the top of Revival. He rigged an anchor in a cluster of small trees a few feet back from the edge. At the same time, Adam and Colby moved to the base of Revival—down right and about five feet lower than the base of Pole Position. The climbers at top and bottom did not have a clear view of the terrain at the other end of the pitch. A couple of trees growing out of the cliff blocked them from merely flipping the rope over to Revival, so Adam untied it from the bag and Jason, still on top, pulled it up. He clipped it through the anchor, tied himself to one end, and tossed the other end down on the other side of the trees. Adam flaked it out on the bag, rigged it through his GriGri and got ready to lower Jason.

Just before starting down, Jason remembers, "It had crossed my mind that we might have added to the rope requirement, so I yelled down, 'Do we have enough rope?' and Adam said something to the effect of 'I think so', or 'I'm pretty sure.' Communications were pretty sketchy because of the wind." [At the time of the interviews, four months later, Adam and Colby did not recall this exchange.]

Adam: "So now I was lowering Jason. My right hand was on the rope, which was all flaked out on the bag, and my left hand was controlling the lever of the GriGri. Colby was standing right behind me. We were joking around, having a great day.

"Jason had descended until he was about 30 feet above us, with his feet approaching a little ledge. I was focusing on him to keep him from tripping over the ledge. Suddenly I felt the 'zoom' as the end of the rope went through my hand. I had no chance to control it. As Jason fell, his feet hit the ledge and he flipped upside down, headfirst. He was not wearing a helmet.

"I was not anchored, and when I saw him falling, just on a gut reaction, I ran and dove at him, figuring I had to keep him from hitting the ground as hard as he was going to. I thought maybe I could catch him—one of those adrenalin rushes. We collided in mid-air, shoulder-to-shoulder, I think. He spun in the air, going from head down to sideways. There's one little spot right beneath the climb that doesn't have a sharp rock in it, about the size of a person in a fetal position, where you could land and not be crushed by sharp rocks. That's where he landed, on his side. He knocked me senseless for a second because we hit pretty hard, but he was knocked unconscious.

"Colby came running over and since Jason wasn't moving at all, we thought he was dead. In 20-30 seconds he came to, with no memory of what had happened."

Church Bowl is 200 yards from the Yosemite Clinic. A nearby climber called 911 by cellphone. Jason was surrounded by rangers and the ambulance crew in minutes. Low cloud cover prevented evacuation by medical helicopter, so he was taken by ground ambulance to a hospital in Modesto, three hours away. He had suffered a broken hip, but luckily his head injury was minor and there were no other significant injuries.

Analysis

As the story unfolded, how many clues did you spot? Did your mind's eye glance down to see if the rope had been retied to the bag?

They misjudged the length of the climb, did not re-tie a knot in the end of the rope, and did not watch the rope end. They also did not communicate their thoughts effectively. Adam agrees that he was ultimately responsible for the accident: "Nobody is kicking himself over this more than I am. I've taught climbing safety to students. How could I not foresee this? It was such a horrible experience for me that I'm willing to talk about it anytime for its educational value."

We see similar incidents in Yosemite every two or three years and those are just the ones we know about. Furthermore, Jason, Colby, and Adam each have several years of experience at top-roping, lead climbing, and rigging and they all climb at a high standard. As Adam says about himself, "Dumb things happen to experienced climbers."

The topo: Revival is shown as 130 feet long and ending higher on the cliff than Lieback. Guidebooks are sometimes wrong, but this should have been a warning. Apparently no one studied the guide closely enough to notice.

All three climbers belayed at least once. Jason says, "I remember...not having a lot of rope left [when belaying on Pole Position], which should have been a clue to me, to all of us."

Adam said, "When I looked at the scene later, it was obvious that we had walked to a lower position [below the Revival belay point], but prior to the accident, we were having a great time and simply didn't notice. When we said, 'just move [the rope] over,' I can't remember looking or thinking that Jason had moved up. Afterward, when I looked up at the cliff…it was quite obvious that there is an elevation gain in the routes on the right."

For a top-rope, 15 feet of added pitch-length needs 30 feet more of rope. Check the math: Does your rope have a mid-mark? Is it easy to see? Is the mid-mark off the ground when the climber tops out?

Despite knowing the rope was short on Lieback and Pole Position, they didn't seem to keep the conversation going. Jason called down to ask about the rope-length for Revival but, perhaps hampered by wind and traffic noise, he did not make sure that Adam knew why the anchor was higher. Colby said, "I knew that [Revival] was longer but I didn't think it was too long for the rope. And I don't think anyone talked about it."

Adam said, "In retrospect, we all have to be willing to communicate and check each other. Little things like, 'Hey Colby, I'm watching Jason right now, can you keep an eye on the rope end for me?'"

Jason added, "Never take anything for granted. You can't assume that everyone's doing his job. I'll climb with people who will check my knots, etc., and sometimes I'll think, 'That's kind of silly, I've done it so many times', but no, you should check and double-check."

The topo effect? Adam: "I don't want to blame it on this, because we should have seen the problem ourselves but I think that when we saw 'top-rope' [in the guide], our minds just shifted to, 'OK, the guide says do top-rope, we'll do top-rope, and we'll be fine.'"

All three climbers are very strict about knotting or tying off rappel and lead lines, but there was never a conscious effort to knot the top-rope at Church Bowl. It just happened to be packaged that way. One reason for an end-knot even when the rope clearly reaches the ground is to maintain good habits so you don't forget or get lazy when a knot really counts—or when you're having too much fun to notice the clues.

Despite his major mistake with the belay, Adam's fast response in braking Jason's fall may have averted a fatality. (Source: Edited slightly from a report by John Dill, NPS Ranger, Yosemite National Park)

WEATHER—FAILURE TO TURN BACK, INADEQUATE CLOTHING
California, Yosemite National Park, Cathedral Peak
On Saturday, November 10, Peter Noble (44) and I, Scott Berry (37), set out to climb the Southeast Buttress (five or six pitches, 5.6) to the summit

of Cathedral Peak (10,911 feet). I had been bagging peaks and leading trad routes up to 5.9 for a few years. Peter, my best friend, had been at it for two. We hadn't climbed this peak before, but we'd researched the route thoroughly and knew it was well within our technical abilities. We also knew it was storm season, but the Thursday evening and Friday morning forecasts called for sunny on Saturday and mostly cloudy on Sunday, with no precipitation in sight. We drove up to Tuolumne Meadows Friday night. A problem with the clock in our cellphone Saturday morning put us two hours behind our intended 0630 start. The days were short now, but we weren't concerned. We planned on hiking back in the dark that evening anyway and even rappelling a few pitches by headlamp if necessary, something we'd done deliberately before.

A ranger stopped to chat as we organized at the trailhead, but we didn't think to ask for a weather update. It wouldn't have mattered anyway. We figured we'd be out before any storm and felt we were prepared if one did hit us.

We carried a double rack of protection, a 60m lead rope, a 60m x 8mm trail line, ascenders, helmets, and headlamps. Peter wore lightweight synthetic pants and a fleece sweater. I had heavy canvas pants and a cotton T-shirt. We both had lightweight wind- and water-resistant soft-shell jackets, which had done well in alpine snowstorms. Should we be stormed on here, our upper bodies at least would be dry and only our legs exposed. We left our heavy rain gear in the car—the first time I had ever done so in 12 years in the Sierra. Anyway, it was only two and a half miles from the base of the climb back to the road, and downhill at that. What could possibly happen to prevent at least one of us from coming out for help?

We started up the Budd Creek climbers' path at 0830 and reached the climb late-morning. Among several variations, we chose the "standard" route, on the left. Our intent had been to haul our packs with the trail line, but the route was too shattered and low angled to keep them from hanging up. Not wanting to carry them all day and to keep them away from marmots, we left them on a ledge 100 feet up the first pitch. It was low fifth-class and we could easily retrieve them on descent. We left our hiking boots, heavy wool socks, lighter, and extra food and water with the packs. I stuffed my jacket into the fanny pack Peter would carry up the climb.

The day was beautiful—sunny with high clouds, warm, and calm—and we did the entire route in shirtsleeves. The climbing was easy and so much fun that Peter twice lowered and repeated pitch 3, the Chimney pitch.

We didn't intend to keep rigorous track of the time, and neither of us had brought a watch. We hoped to estimate the time with our cellphone, but by late afternoon, with one long pitch to go, we realized that the phone's clock was still behind by a couple of hours. There was finally a bit of wind, now—just barely. More seriously, the skies to the south and north were graying over, and long, thin tendrils of darker clouds reached around the peak and drifted over the Meadows under the higher layer. The east was picture-perfect, and a little rain—let alone a storm—seemed unlikely to us. We were only concerned about the time, as the sun had passed behind the peak, and not at all worried about the weather. We debated whether to call it a day and decided that, while neither of us minded retreating at this point, we could probably finish the route if we hustled. I realized, however, that we were committing ourselves to more rappels in the dark than we'd originally intended.

When I reached the base of the summit blocks, I saw a huge, solid black cloud to the west, hidden from our view until now by the peak. The wind was strong and coming from all directions, since the buttress no longer protected me. Peter came up fast and we considered our options, knowing we would not be down before the storm hit us.

We could cross the summit ridge to the usual fourth-class descent on the west face, then descend third-class slopes around the north side of the peak to the base of the route. We knew of this descent, but we couldn't see it from our position and I didn't feel there was time to cross the ridge and evaluate it. Besides, we were more comfortable with a fifth-class rappel than class four of unknown length in the dark, on the face most exposed to the wind, and on the side of the peak opposite our packs.

Our original plan had been to recover the packs as we rappelled the climb, but we now felt we'd be fully exposed to the wind on that descent. Instead we decided to rappel the face just left of the climb. From what we could see below us, several ledges offered good stances, allowing shorter, more secure drops in what was clearly going to be a nighttime retreat, and its southerly aspect might shield us better from the wind. Like the climb, this face was also fractured, posing a risk of hanging up the rope. Because of the conical shape of the buttress, it looked to us that we would reach the ground several hundred feet left of our packs. By this time I had put on my jacket. Peter had inexplicably left his in his pack, five pitches below, leaving him with only the fleece sweater. Neither of us had warm hats or gloves.

The ropes jammed on the first rappel and nothing we tried would move them. We wanted to stay ahead of the storm and we planned to make short rappels anyway, so to save time I climbed half way up to the anchor and cut both lines. We were left with 120 feet of lead rope and most of the trail line. We elected to make short rappels for better control of the rope, so Peter coiled the trail line and lashed it to his back. From here on we simul-rappelled on the lead line, with the mid-point of the rope at the anchor and one of us on each strand. Being side-by-side was helpful. We could hear each other despite the wind and work out problems on the descent.

We descended as safely as we could, using autoblock back-ups between our harnesses and the rope. Each rappel was 40-60 feet.

The sun set and we broke out the headlamps on the second rappel. At this point the cellphone rang. It was our friend Michael. Peter told him we were descending and would return home Sunday. We didn't feel the need for help at that time and were surprised at the good reception. Later, when we were desperate, we could not get a signal.

By now it was pitch-black. The temperature plummeted, it started to snow, and the wind was picking up. Three rappels later we were in a full gale that blew the ends of the rope above us, and the snow turned to sleet, coating our helmets, hardware, and clothes in ice. Ice water poured down the rope, soaking our hands, and we were shivering violently. There was no crack or feature in which to hide. I was surprised that my shirt was still dry under my jacket, but my legs and cotton pants were quickly soaked and stayed that way. Without his jacket, Peter was soaked from head to toe. We joined our lights to scout the route ahead, but sleet covered my glasses and fog cut visibility to 15 feet.

As time passed, my condition deteriorated dangerously: I slurred my words. My vision went temporarily black. I spent ten minutes trying to rig my autoblock, normally a 30-second procedure. I looked for a carabiner for five minutes when there were many clipped to my harness. As we began one rappel, I paused to adjust the anchor, then left the rope entirely unclipped, catching my error just as we stepped to the lip. Peter seemed stronger, taking on chores that confounded me, and I asked him to check everything I did. For the first time, I thought, "We are going to be in real trouble in another hour."

At one point I noticed that the trail-line was no longer on Peter's back. It had somehow detached, leaving us without the option of longer, two-rope rappels or a backup if we lost what remained of the lead rope. We knew the wall steepened below and we worried about dangling on the end of our rope looking for anchors in our debilitated condition. So we now avoided vertical drops and followed ramps and clefts that traversed steeply down and right. Nevertheless, we had to climb to free our rope at least once more. Somewhere below the halfway point, Peter slipped on a slab and swung into a corner. The impact separated his lamp—a detachable model—from its strap, sending the light down the cliff and out of sight.

We'd been using up our cams and nuts for anchors, doubling them up with no thought to their cost. The 14th or 15th drop found us on a slab with no cracks in sight. We were forced to rely on a single, small, marginal cam. As we descended from it, we thought we could see the ends of the rope lying on snow below us. We hoped that was the ground at last, not just another ledge. Halfway down, the anchor placement failed. We tumbled and cart wheeled and I knew that if this were not the last rappel, it would certainly be the last for us. Fifteen feet lower, we stopped in snow and slush, surrounded by snow-covered trees. We were down. We got up, discovered we were uninjured, and laughed it off. I guessed the time at midnight, but it could have been later.

The cliff was a sheet of ice and the wind and sleet as strong as ever. Recovering the critical gear in our packs located 100 feet higher and who-knew-how-much-farther east was out of the question, even if we managed to identify the pitch in the dark. We would have to hike out in our smooth-soled climbing shoes—no jacket for Peter and no way to build a fire.

We had two objectives. First, reach the denser trees along the creek below to seek shelter from the wind. Second, follow the drainage downhill and north toward the road. Becoming lost in this simple topography should be impossible, even in the dark, but any sign of a climber path was obliterated by three or four inches of snow and ice. No matter—parallel the creek, hit the main trail, then the road. Just don't stop. We ditched our gear.

Though sloping gently, the talus slope was so icy that every move sent us sprawling. We walked on all fours, like crabs, over the top of the rocks and into the forest. As we reached the trees we both fell down again, but this was different. We'd been going non-stop for at least 16 hours, we were exhausted, dehydrated, and our legs—not just our fingers and toes—were numb from cold, the muscles barely working. With great difficulty, we got up, trying to help each other, but we both toppled over again. We had two miles to go at that point—on legs that felt like stilts. A log we would have jumped over in the morning required both of us working together to pass on hands and knees. We looked for any sort of windbreak, but there was nothing, so for hours we continued walking and falling, along the creek.

Whereas Peter had held up better than I as we rappelled, he deteriorated faster now and I seemed to rally. He fell more often and stayed down longer. I was still on my feet half the time and I thought we might make it if one of us stayed up. I tried to help him walk, but I lacked the strength to support him or even to grip his sweater. Eventually he simply crawled because it was easier that way.

All night Peter had been rational, even joking, but then he said, in a calm voice, "Maybe we can get some in those shops over there." I warned him that he was hallucinating and urged him to fight it.

We had progressed a little further, when he simply rolled over onto his back. I yelled, "Peter, you have to get up or you'll die!" "That's OK," he said, but he rolled onto his hands and knees and continued forward. Then he said, "Who are all of these people around us?" "They're our friends," I replied, now certain that neither of us would make it. And he said, "Oh, it's OK then." We had moved again a tiny bit, when he asked, "What is that bright light over there?" As I turned to look, he collapsed onto his back and jerked once. A rattling sound came from his throat, then he lay still. I called his name and shook him.

I couldn't check his pulse, since I hadn't been able to feel my hands for hours. I tried to listen for breathing, but I was shaking too hard. For 15 minutes I administered CPR, remembered from Boy Scouts. Finally I realized that, if Peter were not already gone, he would be shortly, and there was nothing more I could do. I was barely standing. I felt the chance of getting out, myself, were slim to none, but if I were to survive I had to leave. Also, I thought—though I didn't really believe this, "If I get down there might be a chance for Peter." I took the phone and car keys from his jacket.

As I was leaving, I noticed the dim form of a tree trunk 30 feet away and I realized it was daybreak. We had traveled hours on hands and knees. It got brighter and warmer as I descended. I was staying on my feet longer and eventually I found the climbers' path, under the snow. Nevertheless, the final mile and a half after leaving Peter was the hardest physical challenge I've ever met. When I finally hit the main trail, I knew I could make it. I was incredibly thirsty. I made straight for the water and food in our bear box, then went to the car. At that instant, I heard an approaching truck. It was a Ranger. I flagged him down. A Park Service team gathered immediately and followed my tracks back to Peter. By that time it was too late. A subsequent autopsy confirmed the obvious: death by hypothermia.

After six months, feeling has returned to my fingers and toes and shooting pains in my hands have subsided. More surprising was the pronounced, though temporary, effect on my left-brain—difficulty with routine calculations, names of friends and family, and short-term memory. I could sense co-workers waiting patiently as I processed my thoughts. (Source: We are grateful to Scott Berry for providing this narrative material, which has been edited only slightly.)

Analysis

The primary cause of this tragedy was insufficient clothing for prolonged and full exposure to the storm. Many things happen in the mountains, even on easy climbs, and can involve experts and beginners alike. Myriad "unlikely" events, including inaccurate forecasts, a late start, a stuck rope, a dropped rack, or a broken ankle high on the route, are secondary to being prepared to sit immobilized and fully exposed to the weather, in any location. In Scott and Peter's case, they started out under-equipped, lacking warm hats, gloves, fleece, and rain pants. Then they separated from the critical gear they did bring—Peter's jacket, their hiking shoes, and fire starter—and left it in a potentially inaccessible location. One key exception to all preparations is that if a lightning storm is headed your way, sitting there is not an option. Descend as fast as you can.

Additional Considerations

The forecast: Weather Service forecasts on Friday and Saturday mornings called for 20-50 percent chance of snow Saturday night/Sunday morning. The forecast is available in the park by phone, 24/7.

The late start: This is not necessarily an issue if you go prepared to climb or hike at night, with a descent plan and survival gear, but if you add any of the "unlikely" ingredients, your risk increases.

The "short" distance to the road: Remoteness should be measured by time, not distance. You can be in serious trouble while in sight of the car and should plan accordingly. (See Yosemite, Royal Arches, V. Madrid incident, in this issue.)

The weather surprise: As we have noted before, there is really no such thing as "bad" weather. The weather you get is what you have. Lightning is always a possibility in locations like this, often hidden until the last moment.

The descent plan: Given the location of their survival gear, reversing the route was their best option, and in hindsight, Scott should have rappelled back to Peter at his first glimpse of the storm. As an alternative, the fourth-class descent was the fastest way out, putting them at the base of the climb in a couple of hours, but Scott and Peter lacked confidence with this kind of terrain. Some critical components of a descent plan are (1) a set of retreat criteria—dark clouds and a turn-around time, for example; (2) a plan for every point on the route; and (3) caution when changing the plan.

Rappel tactics: Short rappels often lessen the risk of a stuck rope, especially in the winds Scott and Peter faced, but this means more anchors and more time are required for the descent. Had they chosen to continue rappelling on what remained of both ropes they could have cut the number of rappels by roughly half.

Losing the headlamp: The best way to carry spare batteries is inside a spare LED headlamp.

Navigating in the storm: After the accident, rangers climbed Scott's and Peter's ascent and descent routes, documenting and recovering their packs and rappel anchors. Because they had been forced to rappel to the right and in poor visibility, Scott and Peter had unknowingly merged with their original climbing route at the top of the first pitch, despite thinking they were hundreds of feet to the left. In a twist of fate typical of disasters, they had climbed a slightly different variation that bypassed that particular anchor, so as they rappelled from it, they did not recognize that their packs lay only 30 feet to the right. (Source: Scott Berry and several NPS Rangers, Yosemite National Park)

(Editor's Note: More details of this incident are available at the website: www. friendsofyosar.org)

FALL ON ROCK—RAPPEL ERROR
California, Yosemite Valley, Royal Arches

On November 20, Meghan (30) and Matt (40), a husband and wife team, had spent a relaxed day climbing Royal Arches (17 pitches, 5.7 A1 or 5.9). Their friends, Greg and Rick, were climbing below them as an independent party. Meghan and Matt reached the top at about 1430 and started down the standard rappel route using two 60-meter ropes around 1500. Greg and Rick followed them down 15 minutes later. This was the first time on the Arches for all four, but they knew from the guidebooks that the descent required some route finding as it wandered down ledge systems. They also knew that it was well traveled and expected it to be equipped with newly bolted anchors.

After several rappels, Meghan and Matt came to a large tree on a ledge rigged with slings and aluminum rappel rings. They were no more than three rappels from the ground with a couple of hours of daylight left, but the way down from this point was not obvious and no bolted anchors were in sight. Was the next anchor directly below, they wondered, or was it off to one side? In Meghan's own words:

"Matt had arrived first and said he looked and didn't see any other anchors and the position of the rappel rings suggested that the last party to use them had continued straight down. He suggested we go the way the anchor seemed to show. The plan didn't feel quite right to me, but it was the end of a long day and I was tired, as I was still recovering from a chronic illness that was limiting oxygen flow in my body. We had a photo of the topo map in our digital camera and we were using the LCD screen to zoom in on the image. If I had been carrying it, I would have looked at it, but since Matt was, and he had already looked around and made his decision, I uncharacteristically did not insist on seeing the topo even though I silently wished to. I decided to just be agreeable, especially since his experience exceeds my own.

"We threaded into the rings. I got on rappel and looked over the edge. Immediately below was a low-angle slab that limited my view to less than 20 feet. Shortly after transitioning over the slab I spotted bolts about a rope-length below. As I rappelled closer, it became clear that they were old button-heads with colored webbing and rap rings interlacing them.

"My ropes had become tangled together [because] the friction from the less-than-vertical granite kept them from naturally straightening. I kept tossing them ahead to determine their reach, but by the time I had them straight, I was further down than I would have liked. The red rope was about ten feet longer than the blue one, right out of the package, and it came within a foot of the anchor, leaving the blue line about ten feet short.

"As I realized all of this, I was within several feet of the end of the shorter blue rope, making it impossible to even do leg wraps with the rope ends to create a friction brake. My options became limited. I was so focused on

DOWN that when I saw a way to reach that anchor my mind didn't deeply explore an alternative—going back up the ropes—that took more time and energy. I thought that Matt could Prusik both ropes off at the tree anchor above so they couldn't run through, and then I could go onto just the red rope and barely make it. I called up to him, but quickly realized the 60-meter distance put me out of sight and communication. I was on my own.

"I was using a Reversino as my descent device, which is slippery for being so near the end of the rope. I tried to tie off my rappel, but could not manage, which is a hint to my diminished motor skills and brainpower. I did not stop and wait for help when I failed at this simple task. I felt I had to do something, and fast. I had a few full-length runners from which to make Prusiks, but I was so tired I couldn't manage to hold my rappel position and tie a Prusik at the same time. However, with one hand I was able to tie a Bachmann knot on the shorter blue rope and clip the sling of the Bachmann to the power point of my harness with a locker. I then deliberately let the blue rope run completely through my belay device so I was just on the longer red line, with the Bachmann holding the blue rope from running away. Still not enough, so I fully extended my Purcell Prusik, which was already attached to my harness power point, and managed to attach it between my harness and the Bachmann to get even lower. After inching the Bachmann a little lower, I managed to reach the slings with my toes.

"I looked up at the Bachmann and saw how close it was to the end of the blue rope and desperately wished that I had put a knot in the end of that rope. I realized it could slip off, but I wasn't panicked. I remember thinking I wouldn't fall beyond the small indentation in the slab six or so feet below the rap station. It wasn't even a ledge. I just imagined myself standing on it while holding the anchor slings. Of course now that my brain is again working with a full oxygen supply, I can see how absurd this thought was. But because it made sense at the time, I continued to operate calmly, although all I wanted was to get my hand on the anchor. So I'm holding the rappel on red with one hand and reaching down precariously toward my foot as it pulls the anchor slings up, trying to get my other hand around the slings. While I was making the big reach down to the slings, the Bachmann must have slipped off the end of the blue rope. I think I instinctively grabbed for it with my brake-hand, allowing the red rope to run through the Reversino. The rope never moved at the top anchor. I just fell off it.

"Months later I still do not remember actually falling, nor do I expect I ever will. My fingertips were ground down to meat, one of my harness leg-loops had melted webbing where it was positioned on the front of my thigh, and the sleeves of my shirt had holes where they fell over my hands. My helmet was unscratched. I recall waking and trying to push myself up, moaning, and then again succumbing to unconsciousness."

Matt knew Meghan was having some sort of trouble. "We were having a hard time communicating over the valley hum," he said, "so I Prusiked my cordalette around both ropes to descend the low angle section in hopes of gaining better [friction.] Just as I got to the transition to steeper terrain, the ropes went slack below me. I heard a scream and the most horrible crash, then silence." The time was about 1600, an hour or so before dark.

Grasping that Meghan must have fallen completely free of the ropes, Matt pulled them up and rappelled from the same tree, but this time angling down a 5th-class gully to climber's right. Matt was constantly calling Meghan's name in hopes of a response. He came upon bolted anchors and from there he was able to rappel another 50 meters to where Meghan lay. It was during this second rappel that he heard moaning from Meghan, confirming that she was still alive.

Meghan had fallen approximately 25 meters to a ledge system less than 60 meters above the ground. "She was on her side in a semi-fetal position with her hands covering her head," said Matt. "I immediately worked to stabilize Meghan's neck, knowing that the fall could have compromised the integrity of her spine. Greg arrived about 20 minutes later and assisted me in moving Meghan onto her back. Greg held Meghan's cervical spine in the proper alignment while I assessed her for injuries. She was conscious but only knew her name. It took about 45 minutes for Meghan to become conscious enough to start piecing together the situation and the events leading up to her fall." (Matt is a Wilderness First Responder and was a past certified Emergency Medical Technician.)

Rick arrived last, rigged a line, and descended to the base of the route. Once on the ground, he ran a short distance to the Ahwahnee Hotel to call for help. The dispatcher at Yosemite's ECC received Rick's call at 1755. She immediately notified the Valley Shift Supervisor and at his request paged additional YOSAR team members. An initial "blitz team" was en route within ten minutes of the alert. They ascended Rick's fixed line in the dark, trailing more ropes behind them so that additional rescuers could quickly bring more medical and rescue gear. Spotlights were positioned on the ground behind the Ahwahnee Hotel to illuminate the scene.

Meghan knew where she was by the time the first rescuers reached her. She complained of significant neck pain, though she did not exhibit any motor or sensory deficits. She also complained of chest pain and shortness of breath and presented with diminished left lung sounds. Her blood-oxygen level was low—90 percent. Finally, though minor considering everything else, one ankle appeared to be injured.

Working simultaneously, Paramedics and EMT-Basics put Meghan on medical oxygen (elevating her blood-oxygen level to 98 percent), established an IV line, and stabilized her spine with a cervical collar and a vacuum body splint. She was given morphine for the pain and was packaged in a litter. At 1955, Meghan was lowered 60 meters to the base of the cliff while attended by a medic, then transported by ground ambulance to Yosemite's heli-base, 18 miles and 45 minutes away, the closest night-time helicopter landing zone. In the meantime the ECC had arranged for an air ambulance to be waiting at the heli-base. By 2145, Meghan was in the ER at Memorial Medical Center in Modesto, approximately 100 ground-miles from the accident scene.

Meghan was diagnosed with a fractured C2 vertebra and a dislocated C3. She had several broken ribs that had punctured her left lung and a fracture of the right foot. However, she suffered no spinal cord damage. It took nine hours for surgeons to repair the cervical vertebrae by fusing C1, C2, and C3. They are hopeful that, following a recovery period of three months or more, she will have little or no long-term disabilities.

Analysis

The Topo: The topo in the camera was a clever idea, but if you're relying on a route map, each climber in the party should have a hard copy. It provides redundancy and lets you to take a quick peek whenever you want.

Meghan concluded, "We were too hasty following the direction the rap rings on the slings seemed to be aimed rather than checking with the topo." It's true that not consulting the topo was a mistake but that should have not played a critical role in the accident. Following the rap rings straight down was actually a logical way to go. One of the more important lessons is that you should not rely solely on a topo. You also need to rely on yourself to be able to recognize and correct a wrong move. In this case that would have meant recognizing the problem and then ascending the rope and starting over. Meghan and Matt had ample time, plenty of optional anchors, headlamps if they ran out of daylight, and two friends behind them with additional ropes.

Fixed Rappel Routes: Why did Meghan let herself get so close to the ends of the ropes? Haste may have been one ingredient, but she hints that complacency was another. "We assumed that on a climb with so much traffic, if there was another anchor it was the right one and that the ropes would reach," she said, "and it wasn't until I was quite close that I saw that the ropes were a few feet short."

In fact, many fixed rappel routes in the park are sprinkled with old anchors and they are often off-route. The right ones may not be obvious and they may not be shiny new bolts. There is no official maintenance of rappel routes in Yosemite, so be sure to have the gear, skill, and confidence to explore and to go back up the rope if you don't find the next anchor.

Why did Meghan keep going at that point? "I thought of it [going back up] briefly, felt ill equipped, and just decided it wouldn't be that hard to go down.

I also had this feeling that I'm an experienced climber, so I should be able to handle the situation. I felt like I HAD to figure it out. I had not thought ahead enough, as I was just thinking one step at a time at this point."

Why did she fall? Meghan again: "As we often do when we are comfortable with things, I had let a couple of key safeties go by the wayside for the speed of multiple rappels. No knots in the ends, which I always used to do! No Prusik on the brake-hand or any sort of rappel safety that would allow me to be hands free. No Prusik cords on my harness like I always used to have." (Ranger John Dill: "With her Purcell and at least one sling, Meghan did have enough gear to re-ascend in our opinion.")

After the fall: It's a big plus that Matt and Greg had medical training. The care they gave Meghan—particularly in stabilizing her spine—may have saved her life.

"It is a bit embarrassing to admit one's mistakes," Meghan confesses, "but also something for everyone to learn from." (Source: Meghan and Matt; David Pope, Yosemite SAR. We are grateful to Meghan and Matt for selflessly sharing their account.)

(Editor's Note: As the rangers stated, "We deeply appreciate their honesty and time in assisting with the re-creation and analysis of their accident. It is our collective hope that all can learn from what they have shared.")

FALL ON ICE, NO PROTECTION, NOT WEARING CRAMPONS
Colorado, North Cheyenne Canyon, Hully Gully

On January 30, moments before falling 170 feet to his death, experienced climber Reid Judson Hunt (32) asked two climbers at a popular ice wall in southwest Colorado Springs if they were done on the "upper pitch," or top part. Pete Elliott told Hunt he and his partner would be finished in about 30 minutes, and Hunt asked if they'd mind if he and his friend rappelled down to climb the lower pitch. They didn't mind, Elliott told him.

Hunt walked to the edge of Hully Gully in North Cheyenne Canyon while Elliott and his friend turned uphill to speak to Hunt's friend, Elliott said. "We turned around a couple of minutes later and Reid had disappeared," Elliott said. "It wasn't clear at first what had happened."

Analysis

Hunt, who was wearing a helmet, wasn't secured to the wall with a rope or wearing crampons, witnesses and authorities said.

Additional Note: Hunt was supervisor of student life at The Colorado School for the Deaf and the Blind near downtown and oversaw athletics, dormitories, and the transition program, said school spokeswoman Diane Covington. He had worked there for three years. Hunt and his climbing partner, whose name wasn't released, are deaf. (Source: From an article by Anslee Willett, in *The Gazette*, Colorado Springs—posted on line)

(Editor's Note: Over the years, we have reported many falls of this type. The climber is at the top of an ice route, not tied in and not wearing crampons, either having just completed a route or waiting to rappel. One small slip in a moment of inattention or distraction results in an unstoppable fall. It is an error that has occurred to as many experts as beginners.)

FALL ON ROCK, INADEQUATE PROTECTION
Colorado, Eldorado Canyon State Park, Roof Routes

On April 22, an experienced climber (24) fell from about 20 feet up on "Kloberdanze" (5.11). As he was trying to clip in to his first piece of protection, his foot slipped, so he fell to the ground. He fractured his left leg. Also of note is that he was not wearing a helmet.

Analysis

Not placing adequate protection on the first pitch is a common problem. It is especially important to do so when the fall is likely to cause serious injury. (Source: Steve Muelhauser, Park Ranger)

FALL ON ROCK—LOWERING ERROR
Colorado, Eldorado Canyon State Park, The West Ridge

On May 14, a climber (22) led "Washington Irving" (5.6), and at the top of the pitch, he clipped his rope into a fixed anchor. His partner began to lower him. When the climber was about 15 feet from the starting ledge, the end of the rope slipped through his belayer's device, so the climber fell 15 feet, injuring his lower back.

Analysis

The lead climber and belayer should always tie into opposite ends of the rope, or else a knot should be tied in the rope-end opposite the leader. In either case, the rope-end opposite to the leader would not then be subject to slipping through the belay device. Alternately, the leader could have rappelled—with knots in the ends of the rope, so he could not rappel off the ends. (Source: Steve Muelhauser, Park Ranger)

(Editor's Note: There were a half-dozen errors similar to this one reported this year.)

FALL ON ROCK, INADEQUATE PROTECTION
Colorado, Eldorado Canyon State Park

In mid May, Jerome Stiller (50), a part-time instructor in Regis University's teacher training program, was supposed to play the "victim" in a mountain rescue exercise Saturday. Instead, he ended up dangling unconscious for real at the end of a climbing rope. He fell about 100 feet, slamming repeatedly into the face of a mountain before his fall was broken by [protection] that held his rope, although his first piece of protection pulled out.

"I hit a lot of things," Stiller said Monday at St. Anthony Central Hospital, where he was taken by Flight for Life. "I must have bounced off a lot of stuff on the way down. I thank God I was wearing my helmet," Stiller said, holding up a dented bloody helmet.

He had broken a shoulder blade, the bone above his left eye, and a small bone in his back and a leg, in addition to multiple scrape wounds. (Source: From an article by Benny Morson, *The Rocky Mountain* News, posted on line)

FALLING ROCKS—PULLED LOOSE BY CLIMBING ROPES
Colorado, Rocky Mountain National Park, The Diamond

Around 2 p.m. on August 7, two climbers (ages unknown) retreated from the Dunn-Westbay (V 5.10 C3). One of the duo was rappelling to Green Pillar Ledge, a bivy platform at the end of pitch-two, while the other climber waited at the anchors above him. Approximately 25 feet above the ledge, the rappel ropes snagged behind a flake, and above the rappeller. The rappeller pulled harder and harder to free the rope. He eventually succeeded, but the flake also tore loose and hit him on his helmet. Knocked unconscious, the climber plunged down the ropes and slammed onto Green Pillar Ledge, where he stopped—a miracle, as the ends of the ropes were not knotted.

Back at the rappel station, the second climber heard nothing from his partner and pulled on the ropes, and felt weight on them. Fortunately, there was just enough slack in the rappel lines for him to attach his device to them and rappel to his partner, who after seven or so minutes was regaining consciousness. After assessing his groggy partner's injuries, the uninjured climber lowered him to Broadway Ledge, then lowered him down the Lower East Face to Mills Glacier at the base.

Fortunately for the climbers, a massive crew of rescuers was already in the Longs Peak area, having spent much of the past week searching for a missing park ranger, whose body had just been found the day before. Other climbers who were also descending the Diamond reported the accident to rangers at nearby Chasm Shelter. Less than three hours after the accident, two rangers met the climbers on Mills Glacier. The injured climber, now coherent, was evaluated by the rangers but refused medical treatment. He did agree to a helicopter evacuation and was choppered out to Estes Park Medical Center. He was reported to have sustained a broken clavicle and several broken ribs.

Analysis

Ropes often jam when the rappel features vertical to slabby faces. When the ropes jam below, one must naturally pull them free to continue the rappel. However, when the ropes jam overhead and out of reach and you are not the last person down the ropes, leave the jam for the next rappeller to free.

It is often easier and safer to free the ropes from just above, where you can easily inspect the jam. Freeing the ropes from the top down also eliminates the chance of dislodging a rock, although there is still the risk knocking rocks onto anyone below. Also, resist the temptation to yank aggressively on the ropes to free them. In most cases, tugging on the ropes will only set the jam even tighter, or, as evidenced by this accident, dislodge rock. Carefully finesse the ropes from above. (Source: Edited from an article in *Rock and Ice*, *#148*, by Duane Raleigh, Editor)

FALLING ROCK—PULLED LOOSE BY CLIMBING ROPES
Colorado, Rocky Mountain National Park, Lumpy Ridge

On August 8, two climbers were descending from a completed climb of Batman Pinnacle. The climbers were rappelling down a loose, talus-filled gully when their rope got stuck. One of the two, (36), scrambled back up the gully to try and dislodge the rope. As he was pulling on the end of the rope, a large boulder dislodged and fell onto his right lower leg. The boulder momentarily pinned his leg against the sidewall of the gully and continued to roll down the hillside. He suffered severe trauma to his right lower leg. Park Dispatch was notified by cell phone of the accident at approximately 11:45 a.m.

Eighteen NPS rescue personnel responded to the accident site. One NPS employee, who is an air ambulance flight nurse during the winter season, worked with Park Medics to stabilize the patient and render medical care. The man's injuries were life threatening and presented rescue personnel with a true medical emergency. Numerous bags of IV fluid were used during treatment due to severe blood loss.

The rescue was very technically demanding and required a short vertical lowering, followed by several hundred feet of loose, low angle terrain. The lower angle terrain required rescuers to pass the litter hand-over-hand across loose talus fields. A Flight For Life helicopter was able to transport the man to a hospital after rescuers carried him for several hours to an open meadow.

Analysis

Lumpy Ridge is an extremely popular rock climbing area in RMNP during the spring, summer, and fall. Some of the finest sub-alpine granite in the United States is found here. However, Lumpy Ridge is infamous for two things: flared cracks that are difficult to climb and protect, and long, arduous, scree and talus-filled descent gullies. This man was the victim of the latter, and while no climber can predict when a loose rock will fall, there are some important points to emphasize regarding climbing and descending safely at Lumpy Ridge.

Loose Descent Gullies. Lumpy Ridge rock climbs are plagued by long, complex descents where loose scree and talus mix with small cliff bands and vegetation. Negotiating this terrain safely after a long hard multi-pitch climb takes great care and patience. While descending these areas, climbers should space themselves to avoid accidentally kicking loose rock and debris onto each other. Descend on independent lines, if possible, or consider tackling some sections one at a time. Loose rock is loose rock, but if care and patience are exercised during the descent, accident potential can be minimized.

Rappel or Down-Climb? The decision to rappel off of a climbing route or down-climb is often obvious due to the severity of terrain; however, sometimes you have the option to choose one or the other. It is important to consider the pros and cons of each and make your decision based on safety considerations and not necessarily on what will be easier or more convenient. At Lumpy Ridge it is often tempting to rappel down all or parts of some of the horribly loose gullies to avoid having to deal with the time consuming task of carefully down-climbing through the rubble. This is often quicker and easier and less mentally taxing. Nevertheless, be sure to consider the cons of such a decision. Rappelling is one of the most dangerous things we do as climbers, so the decision should not be taken lightly. Will the rope knock debris down onto you or your partners as you make your rappel? Will the rope knock debris down onto you or your partners when you pull it for the next rappel? Given that the terrain is low angled and complex, what are the odds that the rope will get stuck when you pull it? Is there a way we can walk around this section so we don't have to rappel? Are the anchors solid? Sometimes the answer to these questions will still lead to a decision to rappel. At Lumpy Ridge, however, make sure you make that decision thoughtfully. (Source: RMNP Rangers)

FALL ON ROCK, FAILURE TO FOLLOW ROUTE, CLIMBING ALONE, FATIGUE
Colorado, Rocky Mountain National Park, Longs Peak

On August 19 about 7:30 a.m., RMNP Dispatch received a cellphone call from a visitor reporting an accident and requesting help on Longs Peak. The reporting party indicated that they were on the Ledges of the Keyhole Route with a woman who had fallen the previous evening and spent the night out alone. The caller stated that she had taken a 200-foot tumbling fall and suffered a severe head injury. The injured woman also told the caller that she had lost consciousness at some point during the night. When rescuers arrived on scene, the woman was shivering uncontrollably and showing initial signs of hypothermia.

Due to the unavailability of helicopter resources, approximately 32 NPS rescuers responded up the six miles of trail and additional mile of 3rd Class terrain to assist with the evacuation effort. The NPS rescuers were assisted by seven Larimer County Search and Rescue personnel and several on-scene visitors.

NPS hasty team rescuers arrived on scene and confirmed that she had fallen approximately 150 feet and sustained multiple serious injuries. These injuries warranted a litter evacuation with full spinal precautions. After assessing and stabilizing the patient, rescuers began directing a litter-carry up and across the Ledges to the False Keyhole. This part of the operation consisted of passing the litter from person to person on 3rd Class terrain for several hundred yards. From the False Keyhole, a technical team lowered the litter 500 vertical feet down to the Boulderfield. A separate rescue team was concurrently making its way to the bottom of the vertical lowering to receive the rescue litter. This team then carried the patient approximately one half mile across the Boulderfield to a helicopter landing zone.

A Flight For Life helicopter from St. Anthony's Hospital in Denver was able to land at the heli-spot and evacuate the patient.

Analysis

The Keyhole Route on Longs Peak continues to be a deceptively dangerous place for mountain scramblers. The route is rated a 2nd Class climb in "Rocky Mountain National Park—The Climber's Guide—High Peaks" by Bernard Gillett. However, this rating can lead to an underestimation of the strength, stamina, and skill required to reach the summit and return safely. The route also contains a considerable amount of exposure at elevations in excess of 13,100 feet, where a fall can lead to serious injury or death.

This woman stated to rescuers that she had attempted Longs Peak twice before but had been unsuccessful due to poor weather conditions. She said that she was determined to make it to the top on her third attempt, even if it meant climbing the peak alone. She was the last person to leave the summit that day and was descending the route late in the afternoon. She ended up in the False Keyhole, a common mistake made by fatigued climbers returning from the summit. Realizing the mistake and that she was off-route, she attempted to down-climb directly back to the correct route. While down-climbing, she quickly encountered terrain that was much more difficult than 2nd or 3rd Class and slipped.

It is impossible to say exactly what caused this woman to slip and fall in this incident. Many factors influence the ultimate outcome of any given accident, and it would be speculation to assert that we can point to them with any degree of certainty. However, some general points are worth mentioning in regards to this type of accident:

Fatigue and "The Descent." Getting to the summit is only half the challenge when climbing mountains. Climbers often spend much of their mental and physical energy getting to the top. However, fatigue becomes a major factor upon descent. Climbers relax their minds and their focus because the goal has been accomplished. The descent, however, is a time for *extra* focus and concentration. It is a time to remember that you are tired and need to remain vigilant. It is a time to keep eating and drinking to keep energy levels up. It is a time to slow down, take frequent rest stops, and watch for hazards. It is a time to pay attention to the subtle trap that is "The Descent."

Climbing Alone—Never climb alone! Right? We have all heard this mantra in the mountaineering world. Yet many climbers and mountaineers relish the opportunity to go solo. No matter what your opinion is on this topic, you should remember never to conclude that climbing alone doesn't involve additional risk.

Summit Fever—"Summit or death, either way, I win." This quote has floated in and around the climbing conscious and subconscious for many years. The ability to recognize and resist this driving force is not always an easy thing to do. Do we climb because we can or because we want to reach that summit? Acknowledging our motivation takes us one step closer to making the decision to turn around for the right reasons; weather, fatigue, route difficulty or complexity, having a bad day, gut feeling, etc. (Source: RMNP Rangers)

FALL ON ROCK, INADEQUATE PROTECTION, OVERCONFIDENCE
Colorado, Durango

After 17 years of rock climbing, bad judgment finally caught up with me. Don't let it happen to you. Climbing near Durango, I was on a route well within my ability and moved about eight feet above a piece of protection, which I knew was probably less than ideal. Thinking, "There's no way I'll fall on this," I continued up. No sooner had I moved up and my left hand greased, followed by my left foot. I slid down the rock (it was just slightly less than vertical), the piece popped and I fell approx 25 feet. I hit a ledge, snapping my left foot. Luckily, I stopped on this ledge and didn't continue to fall further.

I did have my helmet on and lucked out that I didn't fall over backwards, causing worse injury. I suffered a compound fracture of the medial malleolus, severed a posterior vein and artery and a section of nerves on the medial side of my left foot as well as all of my tendons, ligaments, and cartilage on the medial aspect of my foot. My foot was basically hanging off by some skin and tendons on the lateral side. After an excellent splinting job, I was able to hike out to the trailhead with the assistance of three friends and my wife … and with the aid of two chugged beers once I was off the rock. (Hey, it hurt like hell).

I thank my lucky stars I was not injured worse.

Analysis

My mistakes? All amount to BAD judgment: overconfidence, inadequate (poor) protection, and a feeling of "It won't happen to me." Once I am back on the rock, I will be much more cognizant of my mistakes.

I am damn glad I had my helmet on; even though I didn't hit my head, I feel it could easily have happened. (Source: Edited slightly from a report on line—www.mountainproject.com—submitted by Joel Claus, the climber) *(Editor's Note: We always appreciate it when we receive reports in the first person.)*

FALL ON ROCK, PROTECTION PULLED OUT—INADEQUATE PROTECTION
Idaho, City of Rocks National Reserve, Buzzard's Perch

On September 26 at 5:45 p.m., Adam Baxter (24) fell while attempting to lead "Terror of Tiny Town," a 5.11 climb on the Buzzard's Perch in City of Rocks National Reserve. Baxter was about 30 feet off the ground and had placed two cams when he fell. Both devices failed to hold, so Baxter fell into the boulders at the base.

His companions sent for help while assessing Baxter's injuries, which included an abrasion to his forehead, a temporary loss of consciousness, pain in his right hip, and pain in his lumbar spine.

Climbing Ranger Brad Shilling arrived on scene at Parking Lot Rock parking lot to find the patient sitting up talking to his companions, one of whom is a medical intern. The patient refused care, preferring to go by private vehicle to the Emergency Department in Burley. Shilling contacted Cassia Dispatch to advise them of the patient's refusal of either treatment or helicopter transport. The patient and his companions agreed to allow Life Run to proceed in the event that a rendezvous could be possible en route. The patient was clear of the Reserve by about 6:30 p.m.

Note that in the event, the patient did make a rendezvous with the ambulance, and was transported by them to the hospital in Burley.

FALL ON ROCK, PROTECTION PULLED OUT—INADEQUATE PROTECTION
Idaho, City of Rocks National Reserve, Bath Rock

On June 27 around 11 a.m., climber Chris Weber (age unknown) fell 25-30 feet from Bath Rock, causing a compound fracture to his wrist and possible fracture to his elbow, shoulder, leg, hip, and/or pelvis. Belay partner John Fuller described the incident as follows:

Chris was on the 10c route Donini's Crack. He was just below the crux of the climb. He had placed a #1 cam, which did not hold when he took a short fall. After approximately five feet of fall, he weighted another cam that also failed to hold, leaving the belayer insufficient distance to catch the climber's fall prior to hitting the ground.

Within a few minutes, off duty employee Lucus Hengel was alerted to the incident and quickly reported it to CIRO base via radio. Employees Randy Farley and Tom Harper responded. 911 was called and the Almo QRU was dispatched. Life Flight from the LDS Hospital in Salt Lake City and LR1 from Burley were dispatched. Superintendent Wallace Keck was also notified within minutes. Cassia Sheriff Deputy Clark Ward was also en route. CIRO employees were on scene within 20 minutes of the fall. Farley began emergency care, with Harper assisting. Care included basic assessment, oxygen and splinting in preparation for transport. Keck took statements and gathered information.

Life Flight arrived at the landing zone at 12:18 p.m. The patient was always conscious, and did not appear to sustain any head injury. The patient was alert and coherently communicating upon departure from CIRO. No further information concerning the patient was determined prior to this report.

Analysis

Both climbs can be protected adequately though "Terror of Tiny Town" is a precarious layback using very small cams, and Donini's Crack (in the area of the fall) requires utilizing somewhat subtle pods for pro. An above average ability to place and assess the quality of removable protection is indicated on both climbs.

Note that there were climbing accidents in the City of Rocks/Castle Rocks that Park personnel didn't hear about until well afterwards. (Source: Brad Schilling, Climbing Ranger)

(Editor's Note: There are lots of "falls on rock" at this climbing area, which are to be expected given that climbers are trying to climb harder routes here. Most do not result in injury, but many of the ones that do go unreported for obvious reasons.)

FALL ON ROCK, PROTECTION PULLED OUT, PLACED INADEQUATE PROTECTION
Maine, Acadia National Park, Champlain Mountain

The following is derived from interviews with the climbers at the accident scene and an interview with the injured climber after the incident.

Two individuals were climbing the route, "Recollections of Pacifica" (5.9), which is located on the southern wall of Champlain Mountain, at about 11 a.m. on August 20. The climb is a single pitch granite fingercrack leading to a steep slab with a fixed rappel anchor. The lead climber (45) had done this route several times in the past. She was attempting the crux move on the fingercrack climb when she fell.

She had placed four pieces of gear on the route and was attempting the crux move. Her top piece, a cam, was located by her feet. As she stepped up into the crux move, she lost her footing and fell. She watched her top piece come out of the rock, and she fell 15 feet, becoming tangled in the rope and turning sideways and striking her back on a rock outcropping above her partner. Her second piece also failed and came out of the rock. Her partner helped her off the outcropping and untangled the climbing rope from around her.

Analysis

The route where the climber fell is on the central face, to the right of the south wall. A popular climb, it is considered difficult and has limited protection options of small cams and nuts.

This was the climber's first lead fall in over twelve years of climbing. She is experienced and had climbed this route several times before. She would usually place a fifth piece of gear, something she did not do on this climb because she felt it was going so well. Additional protection would have helped limit her fall, and she states that in the future she will always put that extra piece in on this climb. In addition, she was wearing a helmet, which protected her from further injury. Her helmet was cracked in the back and along both sides on the outside while the insert was also cracked.

(Three weeks after her fall she was still experiencing issues with the pneumothorax and has not regained her full lung capacity, but she is hiking and expecting to snowboard in the winter and be out climbing next spring.)

Additional Comments: Evacuation from this area can be difficult due to large talus fields and heavy tree cover preventing helicopter evacuation. Rangers worked with Park trail crew, who were working nearby to repair earthquake damage, to establish an alternate route off the mountain rather than the climber access path. The alternate evacuation route allowed rangers to avoid a dangerous and highly technical route and made a timely rescue possible. Rangers performed one steep angle lower and a second litter belay to evacuate the injured climber via the alternate route. She was then evacuated by helicopter to Eastern Maine Medical Center where she underwent surgery to have her L-1 vertebrae fused. (Source: Edited from a report by Therese Picard, Ranger, Acadia National Park)

FALL ON ROCK
Montana, Glacier National Park, Gendarme

On July 3, rangers from Glacier National Park and wardens from Canada's Banff National Park and Waterton Lakes National Park cooperated in the rescue of an injured climber. The climber, Denis Twohig (68) from Whitefish, had taken a 15-foot pendulum fall while leading a technical rock climb on the "Gendarme" late on the afternoon of July 2nd. His climbing partner stopped Twohig's fall.

The uninjured partner lowered Twohig a short distance to a ledge and secured him. He then left Twohig and descended Little Chief Mountain, reaching the Rising Sun Lodge store about 11:00 p.m. He reported the accident to Glacier dispatch. Recognizing the extreme technical nature of the incident and Twohig's emergency medical needs, rangers held search and rescue planning sessions through the early morning hours to coordinate different rescue options.

After a reconnaissance flight and a briefing by Glacier park rangers, two Canadian park wardens were each inserted via short haul from a Parks Canada helicopter to Twohig's location in the notch of the Gendarme. After Twohig was secured, he was short hauled from the ledge, then transferred to ALERT air ambulance and flown to Kalispell Regional Hospital around 9 a.m. Parks Canada utilizes highly trained helicopter pilots and park wardens for technical SAR missions throughout the mountain parks of Canada. Their assistance was critical as they provided the most viable option for Twohig's immediate rescue.

Analysis

This rescue is an excellent example of the outstanding relationship and true partnership between Parks Canada and the National Park Service at Waterton-Glacier International Peace Park. This relationship is well documented by the Peace Park agreement and is cultivated by frequent contact and cooperation between the two park staffs. Waterton-Glacier is the world's first International Peace Park, and 2007 is the 75th anniversary of the Peace Park designation. (Source: Melissa Wilson, Public Affairs Officer)

(Editor's Note: This report is included primarily because of the admirable international cooperation noted in the analysis.)

FALL ON ROCK, INADEQUATE CLOTHING
North Carolina, Shortoff Mountain, Little Corner

On Saturday March 17, M. McNeely (age unknown) and her husband David, both experienced climbers, were attempting Little Corner (5.6) a rock climb located on Shortoff Mountain at the south end of North Carolina's rugged Linville Gorge Wilderness Area. It was late in the afternoon when Ms. McNeely started the climb, getting solid gear placements as she led the first pitch. She was well into the climb when her hand unexpectedly slipped out of a hand crack. She fell backwards approximately 15 feet striking her back on the rock. Her gear held, limiting her fall. Luckily, her head didn't make contact with the rock, as she wasn't wearing a helmet, which could have compounded her injuries.

David lowered her to the ground. Upon reaching the ground, she had no complaints or concerns about injury. At this point, the couple made plans to climb out, with David taking the lead. However, as the adrenalin rush wore off, Ms. McNeely began to complain of back pain. (She was later diagnosed with four cracked vertebrae). She was also beginning to get uncomfortable and because of her injury and the steepness of the terrain, so she elected not to climb out. This caused the couple to rethink their plans. To compound the situation, the McNeely's were not prepared to spend the night, as they did not have the appropriate gear.

Around 5:30 p.m., David used his cellphone to call Burke County EMS and three of his friends he knew to be climbing at Rumbling Bald, 2.5 hours west of Shortoff Mountain, and asked for their assistance. As late afternoon turned into evening, Marla began to experience back spasms and started to shiver. David started a fire, then huddled with Marla to keep her warm and waited for help to arrive.

Burke County EMS arrived cliff top shortly thereafter, followed by the three climber friends around 8:30 p.m. The climbers met rescue personnel at the top of the descent gully. Due to the limited technical expertise of rescue personnel, the climbers made an attempt to get them to the base of the cliff. However, because of wet and icy conditions in the descent gully, the rescuers felt uncomfortable with this maneuver. Instead, two of the three climbers rappelled to the ground with a sleeping bag and other essential gear and made contact with the McNeely's.

When it was decided that due to the nature of the terrain and Ms. McNeely's condition that it wouldn't be possible to get her out on foot, a Blackhawk helicopter was requested. It arrived around 3:00 a.m., using the couple's fire to guide them to their location. Medical personnel stabilized Marla, placed her on a backboard, then carried her to a site where she could be evacuated by helicopter.

Analysis

Climbing in Linville Gorge is one of the few wilderness areas on the East Coast that offers high quality climbing experiences. Access is limited and demanding. For this reason climbers should be self-reliant and have the appropriate skills to initiate a self-rescue. In addition, climbers need to have suitable first aid and bivy gear with them and be prepared for the unexpected. Rescue teams should be familiar with the areas in which they are expected to respond to emergencies and have trained and experienced personnel. (Source: Les Duncan, Buddy Brasington, and Aram Attarian)

FALL ON ROCK, INADEQUATE PROTECTION
North Carolina, Crowders Mountain State Park, Red Wall

Late in the afternoon of May 13, D. Frank and his partner M. Nagem (45) were attempting a rock climb (route unknown) on the Red Wall. Frank was an experienced climber who frequently climbed in the park. According to park personnel, Frank had led the route and upon descent, had left his quick-draws in place. Ms. Nagem then attempted the climb clipping into the preset gear as she climbed. During a point in the climb, Nagen was just out of reach of the next protection point when she asked Frank for slack so she could clip into the next quick-draw. Frank complied, and it was at this point in the climb when Nagem slipped and fell approximately 20 feet, sustaining injuries to both her left leg and arm, and experienced tingling and numbness in those extremities.

It took approximately 30 minutes for paramedics to arrive and approximately another hour to get the patient packaged and moved off the mountain to a waiting ambulance.

Analysis

In this case Ms. Nagem's fall could have been prevented if a top rope protected her. She could have attempted the climb with this safeguard in place, allowing her to focus on technique, clipping protection, and building her confidence. (Source: Edited from reports by D. R. Tenney, CMSP Ranger, and Aram Attarian)

(Editor's Note: Another incident of note in North Carolina occurred at Crowder's Mountain. A climber was being lowered when his partner couldn't hold onto the rope while lowering him. Evidently, the climber was 40 pounds heavier than the belayer. This has become a common-place incident. The remedy is well known. A belay device designed to provide higher friction for catching heavier climbers and/or attaching the belayer to an anchor to provide better control of the climber, especially when weight is a concern, is the accepted protocol.)

FALL ON ROCK, LOWERING FAILURE—NO BELAY OR BACKUP
North Carolina, Little Pinnacle, Pilot Mountain State Park

On May 23, a group of 35 Boy Scouts of America leaders were participating in high-angle rescue training at Pilot Mountain State Park.

Their activity took place in the vicinity of *Kiss My Ass* (5.8) when S. Richter (23), one of the participants, fell approximately 35 feet. His injuries included a compound fracture of the left arm, fracture to both ankles, left wrist and two broken ribs.

According to A. Whitaker, Park Superintendent, Richter was participating as a "victim" in the training. J. Shelton, Surry County Director of Emergency Services, noted that Richter was being lowered when a "rigging system failed." Evidently, his fall was a result of another participant's inability to maintain control of the safety equipment.

Richter was carried out in a Stokes Basket and transported to Baptist Hospital In Winston Salem, NC via helicopter.

Analysis

When new skills and techniques are being taught in a training environment, extra measures should be taken to safeguard participants. For example, make sure that "victims" and primary systems are backed up. In this case, Mr. Richter should have been belayed.

One statement that was made by an EMS official was that, "When you do a scenario like this there are chances that something will happen." We would suggest that this need not be the case.

This accident is similar to one that occurred at Pilot Mountain a couple of years ago during an organized training session by a group practicing rappelling techniques. In that case a novice rappeller (not on belay) lost control, fell, and was seriously injured. (Source: Edited from reports by Barry A. Whitaker, Superintendent, Pilot Mountain State Park; *journalnow. com*; Thursday, May 24, 2007, "Fire & Police Briefs—Scout Instructor Hurt During Training;" and Aram Attarian)

FALL ON ROCK, RAPPEL ERROR—RAPPELLED OFF END OF ROPE, NO KNOT IN END OF ROPES, DARKNESS, COMMUNICATION BREAKDOWN
Nevada, Red Rocks, Oak Creek Canyon

On February 10, Sheila Matz (50+), RH (Bob), JU (Joanne), MG (Marilyn), PB (Phil), MG (Mike) and JS (Jim) met to climb at Red Rocks. The day was clear and sunny with a light breeze and temperatures in the mid-60's. The Climbing experience of the group ranged from several years (Marilyn and Jim) to several decades (Bob and Joanne). Sheila, although having climbed for 10+ years, did not lead. Jim was a new leader. The group decided to go into the Solar Slab area of Oak Creek Canyon where multiple climbs of similar grades could be found.

Three teams were formed: Phil and Mike, Bob and Jim, and JU, SM, and MG. Hence, three different, three-pitch routes varying from 5.7 to 5.9 could be climbed. All of the routes ended on a large, football-field sized, low angle ledge below the Solar Slab itself, where options existed to either continue climbing higher on the slab or to descend down the gulley back to the base. The party of Bob and Jim finished their climb and arrived on the ledge first. From there, Jim chose to lead a single 5.5 pitch on the Solar Slab proper. Following that pitch, they rappelled back to the ledge area, where they started the seven single-rope rappels of the descent route—the Solar Slab Gulley. After the first short rappel, they made visual and vocal contact with Sheila, whose team had by then arrived on the ledge, and who tried to persuade Bob and Jim to climb back up to join the group for lunch and possibly more climbing. Bob chose to wait at the base of the gulley, since it was already 2:15 p.m. (complete darkness comes about 5:30 p.m.), and the descent would take about an hour to an hour and a quarter followed by a 45-minute hike back to the car. (Sheila & Bob had a dinner commitment at 6:30 p.m.) He was assuming that only one more pitch would be climbed by the teams now on the ledge.

Bob and Jim completed their rappels and reached the base of the gulley uneventfully. However, up on the slab area the team of JU, SM, and MG decided to climb two pitches of "Sundog," a climb on the Solar Slab, which Mike and Phil would follow. Sheila then joined Mike and Phil and rapped off of Sun Dog while JU and MG chose to continue to the top of the climb, two additional pitches. Sheila, Mike and Phil then waited for JU and MG in the gathering twilight. The group of five finally started down the Solar

Slab Gulley in the complete darkness. Two headlamps were produced. Sheila had been offered one of the headlamps, but this was declined.

On the second to the last rappel, MG and JU went first with one of the two headlamps so that they could fix the last rappel, whose anchors were six to seven feet (rappeller's) left of the natural fall line of the rappel. Sheila went third on that rappel, with her set-up being assisted by the headlamp that Mike and Phil had. She had previously rapped the route only once before, about three years ago. She expected that one of the two climbers ahead of her would be at the next rap station with the other light. Unbeknownst to her, both of them had descended to the ground. As she rappelled down, she called out to MG, who by then was on the ground with a headlamp. MG yelled back directions, but Sheila did not understand the response, and mentally was still expecting one climber to be at the next stance. She therefore passed the "unmanned" rap station. In the dark she could not see the bolts or the ropes that hung from them. She continued down and immediately thereafter, the end(s) of the unknotted rope slipped through her descending device.

She fell approximately 20 to 25 feet, landing on her hip in a small depression on a sloping ledge. Had she not "stuck" this landing, she would have fallen another 50 or so feet to the ground, undoubtedly a fatal fall. The impact fractured both her femur and pelvis. Fortunately, the impact did not involve the head, neck or back. Upon landing, she repeatedly screamed, "I fell, I fell." This cry was misinterpreted by Phil and Mike as, "Off rappel!" Mike therefore began his descent.

As Mike was rappelling down, the group finally understood what had happened and Mike, a surgeon, moved down the rap line more quickly so that he could provide assistance. Just below the ledge of the rap station he noticed that he too was running out of one end of the rope; he loudly cursed and also nearly fell. However, he managed to stabilize himself and was able to climb back up to the rappel station. After switching to the last rap line he, and later Phil, reached the victim. Mike proceeded to make an assessment of the injuries.

Meanwhile, below in the valley, Rob V, a climber independent of the original party, was hiking back from his day's exploratory outing and noted a headlamp that did not seem to move. It was 50 feet up the cliff. In the spirit of comradeship that has been a part of mountaineering for more than two centuries, and since he had done some guiding in West Virginia, he took it upon himself to climb up the steep, rocky, climber's approach trail to see if he could be of assistance. Upon reaching the base of the gulley, he climbed up to the scene of the accident. MG, an emergency room doctor, also climbed up to attend to the victim. Concurrently, cellphone contact had been made to 911 and, after being passed through the fire department, was finally connected to the Las Vegas Search & Rescue (LVS&R) Team.

MG and Mike had both done a full assessment of Sheila and determined that there was probably a fractured femur and that there were no obvious neck or back injuries. (Extensive X-rays at UMC Trauma Center would later show their assessment to be correct.) To immobilize the fractured leg, it was tied to two of the backpacks. Additionally, Rob V rigged a chest harness so she could be lowered in the prone position, since she could neither sit up nor be lowered conventionally. With her head and feet being supported by MG and Mike while they themselves rappelled down, Rob V lowered Sheila approximately 50 feet further to the base of the gulley. (The victim's nutpick caught in the rock twice during the descent.)

Prior to the above events, Bob, who had not called in for a "late stay permit," had decided to hike back to the car to prevent an expensive fine and subsequently drove the car a few miles to the highway. After waiting for more than three hours for the non-arrival of his friends, coupled with the arrival of fire engines and an ambulance at the park exit, he was able to confirm the fact that there had been an accident with his group. He then convinced the fire chief to let him drive through the gate with the emergency vehicles.

Upon reaching the parking lot, RH was met by Jim, who informed him that the victim was Sheila. Bob then started up the trail, passing JU, who was headed out to meet the rescue personnel. (JU and Jim had assumed the LVS&R would hike into the scene. In fact they would be helicoptered in.) Soon a helicopter passed overhead. Bob, still on the flat part of the trail, observed the helicopter fly into the Solar Slab Gulley area, turn on its searchlight and hover. It then left the cliff heading back to the road and landed near Bob. Officer Clint M. emerged and spoke with Bob. Clint M. asked if Bob knew anything about an accident and said that a party in the area of the Solar Slab indicated that they did not need a rescue. Bob stated that there was indeed an accident in the Solar Slab area with his party and that the victim would be either on the cliff, at the base of the Gulley, or very close to the base. He surmised that if they had not given the "proper" signal, they might not have known what it was. Bob was able to convince the rescue party to return to the gulley.

The helicopter then returned to the Gulley, confirmed that their help was needed and proceeded to make several more trips in to deposit members of the (100 percent volunteer) Las Vegas Metro Search & Rescue Squad, two at a time, on the edge of a promontory rock. The touchdowns were "one-or-two-skid" touchdowns with a 30-foot drop-off behind the back half of the rotor, while the front half of the rotor was only about eight or ten feet from ground. For added interest, there were multiple trees less than a dozen feet in front of his rotor.

The victim, by this time on the ground at the base of the Gulley, was transferred by LVS&R to a backboard and litter. In the course of the next hour or so, she was then moved another 75 feet farther down the slope to a more clear area where the litter and a LVS&R member, Pete, were attached to a 50 foot cable hanging from the bottom of the helicopter for transport to an ambulance waiting on the road. Once in the ambulance, Sheila was transported to the Trauma Center of University Medical Center (UMC) where the fractured femur and pelvis were confirmed. Surgery took place the next day to insert a titanium rod inside the femur. Prognosis was for full recovery. By autumn she was climbing 5.9 again.

Analysis

As with so many accidents, a series of events chained together the altering of any one of them would break the chain and probably have prevented the accident:

1) Lack of full communication of the expectations for the day. If Sheila had known JU and MG wanted to climb until darkness, she would have descended with Bob and Jim. If Bob had known the full plan, he and Jim would have climbed back up to "pick up" Sheila for the rappel descent of the gulley. (The party had driven in two cars and JU had gotten a "late stay" permit, whereas Bob had **not** thought of doing so, nor would he have, knowing he and Sheila were due for dinner south of Vegas at 6:30 p.m.)

2) Assumptions. In her own words, Sheila made *"assumptions… thinking that they were standard practices for* all *climbers, whereas these were, in fact, only standards for those that we spend most of our time climbing with.* I.e.: *i. Knots on the end of the rope whenever the next belay is unknown, and ii. A person stationed on the bottom of each rappel to assist those who are following to 'land' safely."*

Sheila's assumption that the person with the light would be at the next station was probably key. It had been based upon the fact that this had been the practice with this group for the first five rappels. And, right until the moment she fell, she thought the light *was* at the next station, when, in fact, it was on the ground.

3) Failure to knot the end of the rappel rope. Due to extensive experience with snagged ropes in the tough "live oak" trees of Red Rocks, the ropes were not knotted. Yet when there is no hurry, and there are "extra" ropes available in case of a snag, and when the odds tip against you, such as with nighttime rappels, this safety precaution is even more warranted. (NOTE: Five of the seven raps end on the flat, sandy floor of the gulley, so knots are totally superfluous.)

4) Lack of a Prusik back-up and lack of awareness of distance. Whether a prusik could have "engaged" in the moment between the end of the rope passing through Sheila's hand and belay device is not clear, but it might have provided an additional chance. Sheila knew the rappel was less than 100 feet, but failed to consider that she might be approaching, and exceeding, that distance. However, in the dark, distance is even more difficult to judge. Also, in the natural fall line of the second to last rappel, the "landing ledge" is very small. It is only when one moves to rappeller's left, toward the bolts, does the "ledge" widen to a comfortable place to stand.

5) **Before using rappel ropes, re-set them after an accident or apparent accident!** The person *following* Sheila nearly "bought the farm." When rappelling after an apparent accident, the rappel ropes should be *reset*, as they may no longer be even.

6) **Take an introductory rescue course, or read a book about rescue and then practice**. While the combined climbing experience of the group at the scene probably was close to 100 years, it seemed that no one had experience in lowering an injured climber. Rob V arrived from the canyon floor and coordinated the technical lowering of the victim after the physicians had completed their assessment. True, in this case, the LVS&R could have done the job, but his assistance probably saved substantial time. It is believed that because of the relatively rapid response, the victim, although having lost an estimated two units of blood to internal bleeding, never went into shock. (Source: Robert B. Hall and Sheila Matz)

(Editor's Note: Only a Prusik is mentioned as a back-up. Autoblock systems are also standard protocol.)

FALL ON SNOW/ICE, INADEQUATE EQUIPMENT—ICE AX ON PACK INSTEAD OF IN HANDS, DARKNESS
New Hampshire, Mount Washington, Tuckerman Ravine

On March 31, a climber injured his leg after falling down Tuckerman Ravine. He was with two friends. The three of them climbed Central Gully, hiked across the Alpine Garden, and began descending into Tuckerman Ravine at dark. He was wearing crampons at the time of the fall, but his ice ax was secured to his pack. He said he was not using it because by the time he realized he needed it, the terrain was too steep to take his pack off.

During the descent, he lost his footing and fell between 400 and 600 feet to the floor of the Ravine, injuring his leg during the fall. One friend went to Hermit Lake to get help while the other assisted his friend to the rescue cache near the bottom of the Ravine. Snow Rangers, personnel from the Mount Washington Volunteer Ski Patrol and the AMC, and overnight guests staying at Hermit Lake responded to help the patient. The patient's leg was splinted and he was carried down to Hermit Lake, which involved one 300-foot rope lower. At Hermit Lake, the patient was reassessed and then transported to Pinkham Notch via snowmobile. This incident took 15 people 3.5 hours to complete.

Analysis

If this person had had his ice ax out during the fall, he could have arrested himself and prevented this accident. We often see people descending Tuckerman Ravine in icy conditions without the proper equipment, particularly in the spring. An ice ax and the ability to use it properly are critical for safe travel in steep terrain. The combination of the ax and the knowledge of its use provide a reliable means of stopping oneself on steep snow. (Edited from a report found on the Tuckerman Ravine website)

AVALANCHE, POOR POSITION, FAILURE TO HEED AVALANCHE WARNING, INADEQUATE EQUIPMENT
New Hampshire, Huntington Ravine

On December 20th three climbers were suiting up after breakfast at the Harvard Cabin when USFS Snow Ranger Jeff Lane entered the building. Jeff was in the process of writing the avalanche advisory for the gullies of Huntington Ravine and asking visitors what their plans were for the day. Jeff got into a conversation with two of the three climbers about avalanche stability issues and the Considerable and Moderate postings for the Ravine. Their plans were to climb for a couple of days, with Pinnacle Gully and Damnation Gully as the desired routes, the former being the main goal. With Pinnacle being posted at Considerable (danger for avalanche), Jeff called Chris Joosen on the radio about his thoughts and concerns about a party ascending Pinnacle Gully. Jeff and Chris agreed that that they could not recommend Pinnacle posted at Considerable or Damnation Gully posted at Moderate, but would instead focus on presenting the stability facts. Jeff discussed what gullies had more instabilities than others and convinced them Pinnacle was not a good idea. Although Damnation held the possibility of unstable slabs, they were less likely and not as widespread as areas posted at Considerable. After a 15-minute conversation, they said they would climb Damnation today and perhaps hit Pinnacle the next day.

The weather conditions as they entered the Ravine included snow, light winds, and limited visibility. They decided to head up to Pinnacle to look at it and then traverse over to Damnation rather than head straight up to it. After looking at Pinnacle from below, they traversed under Central Gully and began heading across the top of The Fan. They changed their plans partway across and headed back to follow their original plan to climb Pinnacle Gully. On the approach to Pinnacle, they began pushing through deep snow that they said was up to their chests. They felt that because it was loose and unconsolidated that it was safe and not in risk of avalanching because in their opinion a slab did not exist. When the three were about 25 meters from the bottom of the ice that marks the traditional first pitch, the slope fractured and failed above them just below the ice. At the time of slope failure the first climber was a few feet above the second one and about 10+ feet above the third. KA was out front and yelled, "Avalanche!" and grabbed GW below him. All three were flushed down the slope but remained on the surface, cart-wheeling with the entrained snow. KA and GW were still next to one another about 75 meters below their high point, while KB was sent almost twice that distance farther down slope.

They were extremely fortunate to have no injuries and to remain on top of the snow. After shaking themselves off, they proceeded to search for missing gear and decide what to do next. Two wanted to climb the gully now that it had, in their opinion, been rendered safe by the release of its instabilities. The third was done for the day. They decided that they would all descend.

Analysis

Often it is only in 20/20 hindsight that the causes for an incident present themselves, but occasionally the natural world provides clues that were so obvious they should have been seen and heeded. Each year we have examples of common mistakes that have human factors and psychology behind them even though the natural bulls-eye information was there. This is such an incident. Here are the contributing causes:

Environmental Factors. At 7:00 a.m. the summit temperature was around 15 F with a south wind at 20mph. Approximately 3.5 inches of new snow was recorded at the summit while Hermit Lake in Tuckerman Ravine and the Harvard Cabin in Huntington Ravine each reported about four inches for the same period. Snow continued through the morning bringing another two to three inches to all areas by noon.

Pinnacle Gully is a steep E/ENE facing gully that is cross-loaded by south winds. In addition to spindrift and sloughing from up high, the entire first pitch is water-ice, which does not hold snow. All of this snow piles up at the base of the gully on a slope of increasing angle averaging between 30–35 degrees. This build up of snow accounts for the group's comments of chest-deep snow even though only four to five inches had fallen. The light 7.7 percent density snow and light winds explains their impression that slabs did not exist. Light density snow slabs can be practically indiscernible and although it appears unconsolidated and loose, even the slightest cohesion can create a slab. Slab density closer to the ice was likely increased by the packing of spindrifts and sloughs from higher in the gully. (Pictures taken right after the slide by the group showed constant sloughing from the rock face that forms the gully's left wall, further contributing to the accumulations on the slope.)

Human Factors: Jeff Lane spent 15 minutes of detailed conversation with the party about snow stability in Huntington and specifically the issues in Pinnacle. The discussion ended with Jeff not being able to recommend the desired climb based on instability and the associated Considerable (danger) rating.

When traveling to various mountain ranges that have an avalanche advisory and one is able to speak personally with the individuals who developed the forecast, it should be acknowledged as key data. In addition to avalanche forecasters, there are ski patrollers, guides, Wardens, and Rangers working in local mountains that can provide valuable safety advice worth listening to. While one should not make decisions based 100 percent on the advice of others, it is a good idea to use personal focused advice from experienced local avalanche expertise as a critical tool to help in the decision making process when such expertise is available.

The group initially passed Pinnacle and then convinced themselves that it was okay. It becomes easy to overlook all the red flags when desire overcomes reason. One must enjoy our winter pursuits on the mountain's terms, not on a tight time schedule. It's easy to make a go/no-go decision on the days that are truly nasty or sunny and stable. It's the large spectrum in between these two when one must err on the side of caution and fight the desire to "squeak through" and "beat" the mountain. Snow stability is hardest to assess accurately when the margin of error can result in either a green light or red light situation based on how one is seeing the data. The bulls-eye data can be a little more difficult to pick out. For these reasons, most avalanche fatalities occur under a "Considerable Avalanche Danger" rating.

Safe travel rules were not adhered to and rescue equipment was not worn. Safe travel rules include 1) Travel one at a time; 2) Don't travel over or under your partner; and 3) Have a plan in mind about exactly where you'll go if an avalanche happens. Number three can be very difficult to manage in every situation, but rules one and two mitigate risk well and limit the number of individuals who may be put in a potentially hazardous situation to one. This is absolutely critical to individual and group survival if an avalanche does occur. Having only one person buried allows more individuals to focus on the rescue, thus increasing the odds of survival. On the other hand, having the whole group buried brings the group's chance of survival pretty much down to zero. These climbers were very lucky, as all of them were caught, entrained in the debris, and brought downhill. Had someone been buried, the big problem would have been the lack of beacons, probes, and shovels. If anyone was completely buried this incident would have likely turned out differently. (Source: Edited from a report on the Tuckerman Ravine website. These reports are written by the Snow Rangers: Justin Preisendorfer, Jeffrey Lane, Christopher Joosen, and Brian Johnston)

(Editor's Note: There were several other incidents on Mount Washington, mostly involving hikers and skiers who fell. Two skiers—separate incidents—were caught *in avalanches on Hillman's Highway. In some cases, hikers were wearing crampons while descending. For comprehensive information from the Mount Washington Avalanche Center, go to: http://www.tuckerman.org/)*

FALL ON ROCK, RAPPEL ERROR–RAPPELLED OFF END OF ROPE, NO AUTO-BLOCK AND NO KNOTS IN ENDS OF ROPE
New York, Adirondack State Park, Poke-O-Moonshine

On October 7 about 2:30 p.m., Dennis Luther (40s), an experienced climber, fell about 200 feet to his death from an advanced rock-climbing route up Poke-O-Moonshine.

He was working on a bolted route and then rappelled, apparently with no autoblock, on a doubled rope that wasn't knotted and rappelled off the end of his rope.

Adirondack rock-climbing guide Don Mellor, of Lake Placid, who climbed with Luther for over 20 years, was deeply saddened to learn of the accident Sunday.

"He's a good guy, a good friend of all of ours," Mellor said. "It's a gigantic loss to all of us in the local community, which is really tight." Luther earned great respect as a rock climber and was "very, very beloved by all his friends."

Analysis

For the third year in a row, we have a report of a very experienced climber coming to a tragic end as a result of a basic rappel error. (Source: Jed Williamson)

Additional Notes: Poke-O-Moonshine is a national caliber rock-climbing area, known for clean geometric lines and steep pitch, which makes it popular with advanced technical climbers. There are nearly 150 established "trad" or traditional rock climbing routes up the cliffs of Poke-O-Moonshine reaching 450 feet at the highest point. It is not unusual on a sunny weekend day to see 15 or more groups working their way up the rock fractures.

Poke-O-Moonshine, called "Poke-O" by climbers, has been a popular climbing area since 1955 with famed routes with names like "Bloody Mary," "The Cooler," and "Land of Make Believe."

One other fatal climbing accident occurred on Poke-O-Moonshine on Feb. 22, 2002, when a melting chunk of ice let go under Toronto ice climbing instructor Kevin Bailey. In all, five fatal climbing accidents have occurred in the Adirondacks, three on the loose rocks of Wallface at Indian Pass in the High Peaks, one on the cliffs at Chapel Pond in Keene Valley, plus the above on Poke-O-Moonshine. (Source: All information in narrative and notes from an article found on line at PressRepublican.com, and written by Kim Smith Dedam on October 8, 2007.)

VARIOUS FALLS ON ROCK, INADEQUATE BELAYS, INADEQUATE PROTECTION, POOR POSITION, AND EXCEEDING ABILITIES
New York, Mohonk Preserve, Shawangunks

We received fourteen reports from this climbing area for the year 2007.

Most of the falling accidents were leader falls. Two injuries were the result of falling while bouldering. Protection pulling out and/or inadequate protection accounted for four injuries. In two cases, the belay anchor failed.

The average age of those involved was 34 and the average difficulty of the climbs on which the incidents occurred was 5.6. The level of experience of six of those involved is unknown. Of the remainder, half had none or moderate experience and the rest were experienced. (Source: From reports submitted by Mohonk Preserve)

(Editor's Note: The reports we receive from this location do not contain any narratives. Many of the incidents to which the Preserve responds are minor in terms of injuries, and often the climbers involved do not volunteer much information.)

FALL ON ICE, CLIMBING ALONE AND UNROPED
Oregon, Mount Hood, Southside

On January 27, an experienced Mazama Club climbing leader (65) was climbing solo on the popular Southside route when he slipped at 9,000-foot elevation, sliding about 50 feet before arresting. He suffered a leg fracture during the fall. By yelling and waving, he was able to attract the attention of nearby climbers (including an MD) who provided assistance and notified authorities via cellphone. He was ground-evacuated by a Portland Mountain Rescue (PMR) ready team and AMR Reach and Treat (RAT) team to a snowcap at the 8,500-foot elevation.

Analysis

Solo climbing creates additional risks in the event of a fall or medical emergency. This subject is lucky that nearby Good Samaritans were available to provide assistance. If he had been knocked unconscious during the fall, the outcome might not have been so favorable. (Source: Jeff Sheetz, Portland Mountain Rescue)

FALL ON SNOW, INADEQUATE NAVIGATION SKILLS, UNABLE TO SELF-ARREST—ICE AXES ON PACKS INSTEAD OF IN HAND, WEATHER
Oregon, Mount Hood, Southside

On Saturday February 18, a party of eight climbers departed Timberline lodge for a climb to Illumination Saddle (9,300-foot elevation) where they dug snow caves in preparation for a summit bid on Sunday.

The decision to abort the summit attempt was prompted by the scheduled arrival of a major storm system with high winds (gusts to 74 mph) and 30-foot visibility. At 0930 on Sunday, the group descended on two ropes, with climbers attached at 20-foot intervals, intending to intercept the middle of the Palmer ski lift and follow the lift down to the lodge. They wore crampons, used ski poles, and had a magnetic compass as well as a GPS receiver.

The apparent track of the party was north of the intended heading, and an hour and half after leaving the saddle, the lead climber of the first rope team fell over a "cliff," pulling two other rope team members and his dog with him. The last climber was not clipped into the rope, but holding a rope loop instead, and so was spared from the fall. The second rope team attempted contact by descending about 60 feet over the steep edge, but were unsuccessful. At about 1200 they placed a 911 cellphone call to notify authorities of the accident, before being instructed to "dig-in" at their reported position (as indicated on their GPS receiver.) They also activated an MLU radio distress beacon (exclusive to Mount Hood) allowing rescuers to home in on their snow cave. By 1700, a rescue team consisting of Portland Mountain Rescue (PMR) and American Medical Response (AMR) Reach and Treat (RAT) paramedics reached the five cave-bound climbers who were then escorted to a snowcat bound for the lodge. Part of the rescue team remained at the accident site, descending about 450 feet into White River canyon. The team returned to the lodge after finding no trace of the missing rope team.

The missing party of three (Matt Bryant [34], Christina Redl [26], Kate Hanlon [34]) plus their dog fell several hundred vertical feet until reaching a lower angle section of the glacier. No one was able to arrest, as ice axes were stowed on backpacks. One person sustained a head injury (with signs of concussion), but the other two climbers suffered no significant injuries. The fall survivors did not realize their predicament and continued descending on the previous heading for about 40 minutes. At 1400 the party reached a large boulder in a wind-scoured basin, stopped to bivouac, placed a 911-cellphone call, and activated their MLU beacon. They were reasonably well equipped (sleeping bags, tarp, stove) for waiting out a rescue, although the snowpack was too hard to build a proper snow cave. The dog (a Labrador mix) was credited for helping warm the climbers, but on-scene rescuers observed that it was three-dog night.

Ground rescue teams from PMR, Hood River Crag Rats, and Eugene Mountain Rescue were able to determine the injured party's approximate location, using directional receivers on the MLU beacon frequency. Additionally an Air Force 304th Para-rescue (PJ) team started their way up the White River Canyon toward the accident site, bivouacking at 6,300-foot elevation early Monday morning. Periodic cellphone contact was made with the injured party as high winds and low visibility persisted throughout the night and early morning. At 0600 on Monday, a PMR team descended onto the glacier and radio-located the injured party at 7,400-foot elevation. After a medical assessment and re-warming effort, the rescuers led the party down the White River canyon and were met by a snowcat about a mile from the road.

Analysis

The two-day storm, which arrived on Saturday afternoon, was fully predicted and was known to the climbers. They were confident they could navigate down to the safety of the lodge during the storm. However, their technique was simply for the first man on the lead rope to set the direction of travel from his compass. Without any distant visual reference points, it is recommended that the second person to carry the compass and give "rudder orders" (bear right or left) to the first man while descending. This requires the two be in sight of each other and able to communicate (voice shouts or rope tugs). It is not known why the GPS receiver carried by the second rope teams failed to assist in their navigation problem. If pre-planned waypoints were programmed into the unit, it should have indicated that their turning point (intersection with chair lift) was below them and they were passing above the top of the upper lift station. Their effective track was about 20 degrees north of intended. Also, rather than aiming for the middle of the upper chair lift, it is better to travel toward the middle of the ski area where the three large buildings (Silcox Hut, upper Mile Station, and lower Palmer Station) create a large visual target together with two ski lift cables and numerous boundary ropes. For this track, a slight heading error will not miss the ski area. (Heading from Illumination Saddle is 182 degrees True North).

The icy surface conditions that indicated crampon usage should also have suggested that ice axes be ready for arresting falls. Ski poles are not as effective as ice axes for arresting on hard surfaces.

While the party exercised good survival skills, their navigation skills were inadequate for the conditions experienced (visual whiteout and high winds). This accident illustrates how adequate equipment (sleeping bags, tarps, cellphones and radio distress beacons) can make a big difference in the outcome. (Source: Jeff Sheetz, Portland Mountain Rescue)

FALL ON CRUSTY SNOW—"CAUGHT" A CRAMPON WHILE DESCENDING, PARTY SEPARATED
Oregon, Mount Hood, Southside

On May 20, professional guide Joe Owens (also a PMR team leader) encountered an injured climber at the 9,300-foot elevation being assisted by another guide. The unguided climber (age unknown) had caught his crampon on the snow crust while descending and badly twisted his ankle. The guides splinted the ankle, packaged the climber in a sleeping bag/tarp, and lowered him during deteriorating weather and visibility. The climber was transferred to a ski area snowcat. They also alerted the subject's two climbing partners, who were unaware of the injury.

Analysis

Members of a climbing party must remain in contact (communication) with each other to provide mutual assistance in the event of an accident, thereby permitting the party to self-rescue as appropriate. Professional guides often perform Good Samaritan rescues because of their opportune locations, good equipment/training, and humanitarian attitudes. (Source: Jeff Sheetz, Portland Mountain Rescue)

FALL ON SNOW, "CAUGHT" A CRAMPON WHILE DESCENDING, UNABLE TO SELF-ARREST
Oregon, Mount Hood, Southside

On July 29, a climber (45) caught a crampon tip while descending the standard Southside route, falling about 300 feet. He was unable self-arrest, but as his ice ax was attached to his wrist, it probably caused a shoulder dislocation during the attempt. He also suffered facial abrasions and a sore ankle. With assistance from his climbing partner, he was able to walk down to the Upper Palmer Lift Station where he was treated by an AMR RAT team and assisted down the lift. The subject was taken to a hospital by private auto.

Analysis

Climbers must be well practiced at ice ax self-arrest. If slippery surface conditions, a poor location (run out) or inexperience dictate extra precautions, a rope should be used. (Source: Jeff Sheetz, Portland Mountain Rescue)

FALL ON SNOW—UNABLE TO SELF-ARREST, PARTY SEPARATED, CLIMBING UNROPED, NO HARD HAT
Oregon, Mount Hood, Southside

On September 7, while ascending the standard Southside route, one climber (36) of a party of two lost his footing at about 11,000-foot elevation and fell about 100 feet. He was unroped, unable to self-arrest, and fell onto the lower lip of the bergschrund. He suffered abrasions, puncture wounds, and a twisted ankle. His partner was able to report the accident via cellphone, but was unable to down-climb to assist his injured partner. Both climbers were treated and escorted down to an awaiting snowcat by a PMR/AMR rescue team.

Analysis

Late season climbs are usually more difficult technically, as the snow turns into ice and rockfall hazards become excessive. Under technical conditions the protection of a roped belay is recommended. To allow self-rescue, partners should stay in close contact with each other.

The use of a helmet may have prevented serious injuries. (Source: Jeff Sheetz, Portland Mountain Rescue)

FALL ON ROCK
Oregon, Smith Rock State Park

On Sunday morning, November 4, Jim Anglin (55) was descending into the Lower Gorge by a Fourth Class climbers' way at the southeast end of Smith Rock State Park when he lost his footing and fell about 100 feet to his death. No one saw him slip. Anglin and his climbing companions had been heading down into the Lower Gorge to climb traditional routes in that area of the Park.

Analysis

Jim Anglin had been rock climbing at the highest level at Smith Rock since the 1980's, and is credited with many first ascents. Recently, he had participated in replacing anchors on routes on Monkey Face.

The Fourth Class Climber's Way they used on Sunday descends into the Gorge from a section of the volcanic Rim Rock located behind the Park Offices. This hard basaltic rock does not degrade into the slippery-gravel over sloping-rock base that is typical of Welded Tuff rock, according to Smith climber Ian Caldwell. Hiking trails elsewhere in Smith Rock State Park and climbs in other volcanic areas in Central Oregon, such as Three Fingered Jack, have this dangerous slippery-gravel condition.

Reportedly, his companions did not see what caused him to fall.

The Climber's Way into the Lower Gorge is described as a Fourth Class descent slot by Alan Watts on page 234 of his "Climber's Guide to Smith Rock." Fourth Class climbing requires balance, care, and the use of hands and obviously may involve serious injury or death if a fall should occur. (Source: Robert Speik)

(Editor's Note: We are reminded that sometimes in familiar and what might be considered benevolent terrain, even the best of climbers can experience an accident.

A final note regarding the February 2006 fatalities on Mount Hood reported in last year's ANAM. Jeff Sheetz sent forward the following: "As a direct consequence of this high profile search, the Oregon state legislature is proposing bills that mandate electronic signaling devices (such as Personal Locator Beacons, Mountain Locator Beacon, GPS receiver with cellphone, and two-way radios) for all climbs above 10,000 feet on Mount Hood. Most local rescue personal and climbers encourage the use of such equipment but do not believe its use should be required. For this particular accident, the stormy weather delayed reaching even known locations in the summit area, so electronic signaling would not likely have affected the outcome.

"Several organized searches were conducted during the summer of 2007. A very large equipment cache containing sleeping bags, bivy sacks, stoves, extra clothes,

a shovel, a backpack, and other equipment was found in the hut where the party stayed. Essentially, all of their survival equipment was left behind early on the approach. The upper sections of the Newton-Clark and Eliot glaciers were searched by air and ground teams, but no additional clues as to the fate of the two missing climbers were found.

"It should also be noted that the climbers left their vehicle on December 7, not December 6. This provides at least a partial explanation why they were late starting on the route—as further evidenced by the photos recovered.")

FALL ON ICE, GEAR RACKED RANDOMLY, FATIGUE, FAILURE TO LISTEN TO INSTINCTS, POSSIBLE SENILITY
South Dakota, Spearfish Canyon

February 6. Aging ice climber (67) begins approach too tired to get to base of climb (100 feet from road), but with the aid of ski poles manages anyway. Almost senile, climber fails to rack his ice screws so as to easily get at them on harness. (Left them random racked randomly on shoulder sling.) Three or four screws up (leading), finally notices, but decides too much trouble to deal with. By now terrain is vertical. Creeping senility (also name of favorite rock climb nearby) still allows awareness of much-increasing tiredness. About four or five feet above last ice screw, whacking in ice tool, thinking probably good enough (really tired now), but knowing it could be better. Whacking away (limply) with second tool and not getting it to seat. Whack again, and... POP! He is off. (Gee, it sure was fast!) Right foot hits steeply sloping ledge about one-foot wide. Crampons catch. Ouch.

Good belay a foot or so farther brings old climber up just fine. (Belayer is EMT for local ambulance crew.) Not to be deterred (sure sign of arrived senility), climber climbs back up to give it another go, but notices (about three feet above the last saving ice screw) that his foot still hurts and he can't really put weight on it. So, back down, then a lower to the ground. Belayer (fortunately not senile or out-of-it) looks at foot and says, "Hmmm...," then retrieves gear.

Analysis

Good foresight shown by climber in bringing ski poles for the lengthy approach, because they are much needed on the way out. Maybe not senile after all. (Source: Written by the not-so-senile climber after all, Peter Lev)

FALL ON ROCK—IMPROPER USE OF HARNESS (TIED INTO GEAR LOOP), INADEQUATE PROTECTION, INADEQUATE BELAY, INEXPERIENCED
Texas, Reimers Ranch County Park, Dead Cat's Wall

On November 18, three adults acting as guides took six teenagers on a church youth group trip to Reimers Ranch, a central Texas limestone sport climbing area popular for its concentration of moderate climbs. The group leader,

Kyle Focht, had six years of climbing experience and had taken groups on similar outings in the past. Official guides to the area are somewhat unusual, and youth groups led by an experienced leader are a common sight at the park. The group climbed at a popular beginner's wall known as Dead Cat's, a 35-foot cliff that is frequently climbed and typically crowded. Climbing at Reimers Ranch is done in a canyon along the Pedernales River. Trail access is a steep trail through a limestone creek bed. Approaches at the park are quite short, but the trails are steep and varied.

As the day was winding down Emily Jackson (17) led a thirty-five foot 5.10 route called Hello Kitty. Hello Kitty has three bolts and a two-chain anchor system. She was belayed by another group leader, Jason Weaver (26), who had about a year of experience belaying. Jason chose to anchor himself to a tree with webbing as "an extra safety measure." Emily had been climbing for about one year and had successfully cleaned this particular route several times. Prior to starting this climb, Emily was asked if she felt confident to clean the route. She said that she did and recited the process of cleaning to the group leader.

When Emily reached the top of the route, she prepared to clip directly into the anchors. On her harness were two 60-cm slings of one-inch webbing, one looped through her belay loop, the other clipped to a gear loop with two carabiners. Emily clipped into the chain with the carabiner that was attached to her gear loop rather than the one fixed through the waist of her harness. It is unclear whether Emily didn't notice the error or if she believed it was safe. After clipping in with the single sling, Emily had her belayer test the weight. It held, and she came off belay and untied from the rope. The gear loop held for much of the cleaning process. When she prepared to retie into the rope, the gear loop broke, and Emily took a ground-fall.

The belayer, uncertain if she was tied back in yet, pulled the rope tight. He attempted to rush forward and guard her fall, but being anchored to the tree was not able to move. Emily landed feet first, bounced backward onto her tailbone, and continued to fall down the hill behind the trail. She came to a stop when she somersaulted into a boulder.

When Focht, Weber, and a woman who said she was a nurse came to her, Emily was unconscious for less than a minute. A member of the nurse's group went to call 911. Emily was not moved. Focht and Weber checked vitals and spoke to her while they waited. EMS arrived, and Emily was lifted out by helicopter. During the rescue and attending commotion, the rest of the group was supervised and kept calm by the third group leader. Emily's injuries included a broken right hand, a bruised lung, and scratches. Remarkably there was no head, neck, or back damage. She spent the night in a hospital in Austin.

Analysis

Group climbing outings are common at parks such as Reimers Ranch, where easy approaches and moderate climbs draw beginners. These outings are often well supervised, fun, and educational. This accident was the result of several factors, mainly inexperience and a lack of knowledge about gear.

First, the climber in this instance did not follow the usual technique for anchoring directly to the wall. Most climbing instructors and manuals advise clipping into both sides of a typical chains and bolts anchor system. Redundancy is a key aspect of a safety system. The climber in this case made only one connection with the anchor.

Secondly, it is unclear what measure of safety was intended by anchoring this belayer to the tree. When a belay station is unstable or a belayer is significantly outweighed by the climber, anchoring while belaying on the ground is useful. In this instance, it may have impeded the belayer's ability to react to the fall and possibly arrest the secondary fall that caused further injury.

Both of these factors are matters of training, experience, and style. The climber in this instance had been trained to anchor at only one point.

The most important factor in this accident was knowledge of gear. Not all harnesses are created equal. There are several harnesses on the market whose gear loops are weighted to take a fall. It is not the typical design, however, and it is the climber's responsibility to be familiar with their harness and rack their gear accordingly. Emily was using a MadRock Venus harness that had been purchased new two months earlier. The Venus' belay loop is rated to take a 26kn, its haul loop is rated for 24kn. Both of these loops can take typical lead falls for several years before these limits are compromised. The gear loops of the Venus, however, are rated for 5kg, and not intended to hold weight beyond the standard load of gear.

It's unclear what the intent of the extra sling on Emily's harness was. For a simple sport climb like this, there would be no need to make a runner or use a sling as an extra long draw. Climbing partners of any experience level ought to check each other's protection system and point out any extraneous, improperly racked, or conspicuously absent gear. Had Emily removed this extra sling altogether and only clipped into the anchor chains with the sling attached to her belay loop, she would have been secure at the anchor.

Additional Comments: Since 2004, the Central Texas Mountaineers climbing club in Austin has replaced chain-only anchors with sport anchors/permanent clips on the more popular routes at Reimers Ranch. These sport anchors eliminate the need for a climber to untie and re-thread the rope to clean draws. Hello Kitty, although it is in the more popular part of the park, had not yet had sport anchors installed on it.

Cleaning a route is a common scenario for accidents, often resulting in more severe injuries than happened in this instance. But the wider use of sport-clips could both alleviate and exacerbate the problem. With sport anchors in place, climbers never disconnect from their belayer, and falls such as this will not occur. However, climbers who use only the sport anchor system will not learn proper cleaning technique for chain anchors and will not be comfortable with the procedure should they face it later on. As they advance to harder routes or travel to climb, they will encounter anchor systems that require them to disconnect from the rope and rely on a personal anchor system. Always be aware of what type of fixed gear is present on a route, and use verbal commands whenever possible to guide your partners through new skills and procedures. (Source: Ann Raber, Reimers Ranch Climbing Committee)

AVALANCE, POOR POSITION
Utah, Little Cottonwood Canyon, Pfeifferhorn

On February 3, Brian Dutton (42) and Joe Bullough (42) attempted to climb the East Ridge of Pfeifferhorn on the Little Cottonwood/American Fork ridgeline at 11,326 feet. On the East Summit Ridge, they triggered a small, hard, slab avalanche three to six inches deep and 70 to 100 feet wide. The avalanche carried them off the south side of the peak, running 700 vertical feet into Dry Creek Canyon in Utah County. Neither climber was buried, but they were carried over 150-foot cliff bands and sustained major injuries. Fortunately, Dutton was able to get to his cellphone out and call 911.

Rescuers responded from Wasatch Backcountry Rescue, Utah County SAR and Salt Lake County SAR. A team started skiing in from White Pine Trailhead just before 11 a.m. and reached the victims three hours later. Winds of 50 to 90 mph made the route along the Pfeifferhorn ridgeline extremely difficult. The patients' injuries and the remote location ruled out anything other than helicopter evacuations. Both patients were treated at the scene, and then transported by ski toboggan further downhill to a suitable LZ. Despite the wind, Life Flight was ultimately able to land at the LZ before dark and transport both of them to the hospital.

Analysis

Climbers need to be just as focused on avalanche conditions as backcountry skiers are. For climbers in exposed terrain, the consequences of being caught can be very high, even for a small avalanche. The summit ridge of the Pfeifferhorn is often wind scoured, but this particular storm had loaded it with fresh deposits. (Source: Tom Moyer, Salt Lake County Sheriff's Search and Rescue)

FALL ON ROCK, PROTECTION PULLED OUT—QUALITY OF ROCK
Utah, Little Cottonwood Canyon, Hellgate Cliffs

On August 4, Daniel Filler (21) suffered a 15 to 20 foot ground-fall at Hellgate Cliffs in Little Cottonwood Canyon. He was climbing Dark Star (5.12a), a trad route on a crag otherwise full of bolted climbs. He had placed three pieces when he fell. The third piece, a large nut, pulled when it was loaded. He hit the ground, landing on rocks and bushes.

Salt Lake County SAR and Unified Fire responded. They packaged Daniel in a litter and vacuum splint and lowered him down the scree slope to the trailhead. He was then transported by ambulance.

Analysis

Hellgate Cliffs are a limestone outcrop in Little Cottonwood. This area is known for rockfall and pulled holds. It is likely that poor rock quality contributed to the failure of the nut placement. (Source: Tom Moyer, Salt Lake County Sheriff's Search and Rescue)

FALLING ROCKS—DISLODGED BY PULLING ON ROPE
Utah, Little Cottonwood Canyon, Church Vaults

On September 3, Gary Wholfarth (43) and two friends had been climbing in the Church Vaults area of Little Cottonwood Canyon. In the process of pulling their rope after a climb, it became stuck in the rocks. When they pulled hard on the rope to free it, several large rocks were dislodged. One of them hit Gary in the head, injuring him despite the helmet he was wearing. One friend ran down the trail to the road to call for help while the other started walking Gary down the trail. Before SAR team members had arrived, the two climbers reached the road and Gary was transported by ground ambulance to the hospital.

Analysis

Any time a rope is being pulled, rockfall is a possibility. Wearing a helmet is always a good idea, but it's also best to move out of the line of fire before pulling. In most places it is possible to pull from a location other than directly under the rope. (Source: Tom Moyer, Salt Lake County Sheriff's Search and Rescue)

(Editor's Note: There were a few other accidents in Utah this year, most notably an ice climbing fatality on Bridal Veil Falls in Provo Canyon. No details were available other than that it was a 32-year-old man who fell 200 feet.)

LOSS OF CONTROL—VOLUNTARY GLISSADE, FAULTY USE OF CRAMPONS
Washington, Mount Adams

On June 24, a climber (38), who had summited Mount Adams alone, was descending wearing crampons when the points on the right crampon "caught" his left leg, causing him to fall and resulting in a broken ankle.

He was assisted down by a group of climbers until Tacoma Mountain Rescue Unit evacuated him on a Cascade litter. It involved multiple lowers. A lengthy transport by a wheel litter brought him to the road head, where two "Good Samaritans" transported him to Seattle. Klickitat Search and

Rescue and Central Mountain Rescue assisted. (Source: Berndt Bittling-meier, TMRU)

Analysis

Once again we have a climber who makes the wrong decision: glissading with crampons. (Source: Jed Williamson)

FALL ON ICE–CAUSED SHOULDER DISLOCATION
Washington, Mount Rainier, Kautz Glacier

On July 25th, the fifth day of a successful expedition via the Kautz Glacier route, a client with International Mountain Guides suffered a shoulder dislocation during a short fall while descending from high camp back to the parking lot. At 12:10 p.m., four guides were leading eight clients down "The Turtle" snowfield (part of the Kautz Glacier approach route) at approximately 10,000 feet when the accident occurred. The team was divided into four rope teams of three, each with two clients and one guide.

At the time of the incident, the weather was clear and sunny and the temperature was mild. The team had spent the morning packing up camp and waiting for the snow to soften, which usually makes downhill travel easier on the knees. By the time the group descended, the snow had softened enough to allow plunge stepping in most areas; however, small patches of hard snow and ice still existed in some places. Climbers would warn each other when icy patches were discovered so that the next person moving through the area could avoid a potential slip.

The climbers were wearing light clothing layers and carrying heavy multi-day packs. The terrain was benign (20 degrees) in comparison to the technical sections of the Kautz Glacier Route that the group had already climbed. The snowfield both above and below the accident site was slightly steeper than 20 degrees, and each team of clients was being short-roped. This is done with the guide at the upper end of the rope with short, tight distances between each of the two clients on the rope below. In this way, the guide can more easily catch a slip or note fall before momentum is gained.

The accident occurred when the client on the front of one rope slipped on a patch of ice while descending and yelled, "Falling!" The second/middle climber went into self-arrest. Together they slid only a short distance before coming to a stop. The front climber jumped up uninjured, but the middle climber remained prone in the snow. Another rope team was very close, which allowed two guides to perform a quick visual and physical assessment of the patient and the injury. They determined he would be able to walk but that he needed assistance with the heavy pack. They regrouped at a safe rocky area nearby in order to further assess the injury and figure out a way to approach the rest of the descent.

The client was responsive and showed little signs of discomfort other than favoring his right arm. He explained that as he dropped into self-arrest, his heavy pack pulled hard across his back and contributed to the pain he felt in his left shoulder. After a more detailed assessment, he also indicated that he only felt a small amount of pain on the inside of his bicep and had a limited range of motion. Otherwise, he was fine, had a positive attitude, and showed no other signs of injury.

The guides decided that he could continue the descent to Paradise unassisted, but only with a very light pack—no more than ten pounds. Everybody agreed to continue this way, and it took the group about four more hours to reach Paradise. The guide continued to check on him during the descent and reported that he was doing fine and had no additional pain or discomfort.

Once at Paradise, the climber was transported to a hospital for an X-RAY. There, the doctors found a dislocated shoulder. The climber was treated and released that day.

Analysis

Dislocated shoulders are one of the most common injuries on Mount Rainier. A shoulder dislocation can be difficult to detect sometimes, as this incident shows. However, if left untreated, dislocated shoulders can lead to long-term disabilities in the arm. Fortunately for this climber, doctors were able to reduce the injury, and he walked away without any serious complications. Based on the information the guides had during the incident, there wasn't a compelling reason to risk a helicopter flight. (Source: Mike Gauthier, Climbing Ranger)

FALL INTO CREVASSE (BRIDGE COLLAPSE)—DISLOCATED SHOULDER
Washington, Mount Rainier, Emmons Glacier

On July 28th, an RMI client (38) fell a short distance into a crevasse, sustaining a shoulder dislocation while descending the Disappointment Cleaver Route. The fall was apparently due to a bridge collapse or partial bridge collapse. The incident occurred on the Emmons Glacier close to where the Emmons and Ingraham glaciers diverge (12,300 feet) at approximately 12:15 p.m. The route the guide services were using had just recently changed course slightly; therefore, it was a new crossing.

Burdick was not hanging more than ten feet into the crevasse, and the guide service easily extracted him by hand. An RMI guide completed a patient assessment, and a posterior shoulder dislocation was the only injury found. Burdick was otherwise in good shape and had a positive attitude. The guide then notified other guides at Camp Muir of the situation. The guides at Camp Muir notified the climbing ranger at Camp Muir of the incident. RMI requested a helicopter for evacuation. A ranger team at Longmire was organized and a military Chinook was ordered to the Kautz helicopter base in Mount Rainier National Park. The request was put in at approximately 1:30 p.m.

An attempt at relocating the shoulder proved futile, so the guides on scene stabilized and packaged the shoulder in the position found. The preferred method would have been to evacuate Burdick at the incident site, but the helicopter notified the Park Service that it would take at least two hours to reach Kautz helicopter base. The air mission adviser decided it would be safer to evacuate the patient from a flat landing zone some 1,000 feet below known as the "Football Field" (just below the Cleaver). It took a total of four guides to safely walk Burdick to the designated landing zone. Two more guides were needed from Camp Muir to assist in escorting the remaining clients back to camp.

The Chinook helicopter was on the ground at Kautz helicopter base before guided team could make it to the Football Field, giving the ranger just enough time to brief the flight crew and pilots. Burdick arrived at the Football Field at 4:35 p.m. and was extracted by helicopter at 5:05 p.m. via a ground landing. Burdick was back at Kautz at 5:07 p.m. and transferred to an American Medical Response ambulance for transport to Good Samaritan Hospital in Puyallup. The incident was successfully completed well before nightfall with all field teams back at Camp Muir.

Analysis

Rescues like this show how easy and non-threatening these situations can be under the right circumstance. Note that skilled guides and planned communication considerably affected the response. RMI used additional personnel at Camp Muir who were able to help as the summit team arrived (after the rescue was over) back late in the evening. Also, the NPS was able to assemble a flight team and high altitude helicopter on short notice. Most notably, an US Army flight crew for a Chinook helicopter came in on their off- day (in under two hours) to assist climbers in distress. These factors, all in place, were what made for a safe and efficient rescue response. (Source: Mike Gauthier, Climbing Ranger)

FALL ON ROCK, WRONG TYPE OF BOOTS, NO SPOTTER
Washington, Washington Pass, Liberty Bell
I have been climbing since the early 1950s and still get out to unexplored areas these days. After climbing in an untouched area of the Pantheons in the BC Coast Range, Mickey Schurr and I headed off to do some classic climbs in the Cascades. There I came-a-cropper for the first time.

Before noon on August 5, Mickey and I began hiking up the Blue Lake trail at Washington Pass. We reached the final 5.7 slab pitch of the Beckey Route on Liberty Bell between three and four o'clock. This pitch is short and is usually done without placing protection. Three-quarters of the way up I slipped, injuring my right ankle. The summit was near and Mickey led the pitch wearing his kletterschuhe. I followed, but a clap of thunder and raindrops after I reached the top of the slab showed that thunderstorms from the east were on us, so we retreated. Discomfort was OK, but lightning danger wasn't. A short rappel carried us below the slab and two single-rope rappels took us to the notch.

My descent was slow, but we reached the trail before dark. Mickey was a steady and helpful companion, and I picked up my trekking poles where I stashed them in a meadow, but even so, it was eleven o'clock before we reached the parking lot. There was light rain and distant thunder for most of the return. We drove to Seattle the next day, after spending the night at the Colonial Creek Campground. The emergency room at Northwest Hospital diagnosed a broken right medial malleolus, skillfully set by Herbert Clark, MD, using four screws.

Analysis
Wearing kletterschuhe rather than boots, better technique, and having Mickey spot me while making the move would have avoided this unpleasantness. I have often wondered, "What would happen if I were to fall here?" when I was in some unprotected spot. I conclude that it is better that you should never have occasion to find the answer to this question. (Source: Former AAC Safety Committee member, Peter Renz)

LOST—WEATHER, INADEQUATE EQUIPMENT
Washington, Mount Rainier, Muir snowfield
On Sunday, September 16th at 6:00 p.m., Chris Stanko and Alex Mondau contacted a Park Ranger at Paradise and reported that their partner Phil Michael was overdue. The pair had just returned from Camp Muir earlier in the day. The party of three originally arrived at Camp Muir on September 14th. Michael and Mondau successfully climbed to the summit on the 15th and returned to Camp Muir for the night. Michael was reportedly doing very well but took extra time visiting with climbers at Camp Muir. Stanko and Mondau told the ranger that they had separated from Michael at about 11:30 a.m. near Moon Rocks (8,900 feet) on the Muir Snowfield while descending in poor weather. So when Michael did not show up at Paradise by late in the day, Stanko and Mondau became concerned but were confident he'd come out on his own in the morning. They said that Michael was an experienced climber and international mountain guide who was very resourceful and skilled, and that he was carrying overnight equipment and food.

Monday, September 17th. When Michael did not return, Stanko and Mondau contacted a park ranger again and completed a lost person questionnaire. Climbing rangers were notified and hasty search teams were assembled. Three teams were sent into the field; two were assisted by Stanko and Mondau. These teams ascended in a search pattern from Paradise to the point last seen. Each team searched different areas on the descent. Throughout the day, the weather remained poor, visibility was limited, and there was rain mixed with snow. Searching revealed no clues, and Michael was not found. All search teams returned from the field at 7:00 p.m. They were sent home and asked to prepare for another day of searching.

Earlier in the afternoon a seemingly different incident developed. Chuck Cruise contacted the Park Service at 12:30 p.m. and reported that his fellow employee Michelle Delorenzo had not shown up for work that morning. She had left information with Cruise stating her plans were to go hiking at Mount Rainier with her friend "Brian." This report was received at the Mount Rainier Communications Center. Park Rangers were notified, and they looked for a vehicle as described by Cruise. It turned out that Cruise had the wrong vehicle information so the correct vehicle wasn't determined until later in the day. This made it difficult to ascertain whether Delorenzo and her friend Brian were actually in the park. Later Delorenzo's registration was located and it was discovered that a person named Lance had registered the two of them (not Brian). Finally, the correct vehicle could be located, and it was indeed in the Paradise lot. The connection was not made until late in the day. The Park would be searching for three people from two separate parties the next day.

Tuesday, September 18th. The Incident Command Team met at 6:00 am and briefed the search teams for a second day of searching. Eight ground teams were given assignments and a helicopter was put on standby (at the time, the weather was poor but forecast to improve). While the search teams were en route to their respective search zones, one team located Michael, Delorenzo, and Lance. They were found near Panorama Point at about 7,000 feet and descending toward Paradise. They were in good shape, without injury, and able to walk out on their own.

Analysis

After separating from Stanko and Mondau, Michael heard people calling for help to the west. Michael started in the direction of the calls and in a short time found Delorenzo and Lance. At the time, the visibility was very poor with fog and rain, leaving anybody without shelter very exposed and wet. Delorenzo and Lance hadn't made it very far before they became lost on the Muir Snowfield. Michael found them both cold, wet, and without a tent. (They had spent the previous night in the Muir public shelter).

Delorenzo noted that the boot track down from Camp Muir was very difficult to follow. The upper Muir Snowfield was actually hard, dirty ice, which did not allow for fresh boot prints, as is also the case with soft snow. Rain and the high humidity associated with the fog caused any tracks to melt very quickly. After a few hours of trying to find the trail, the pair realized they were lost and in a precarious situation. That was when Michael arrived.

Michael attempted to lead the group back to the primary descent route, but the weather continued to deteriorate, and he too was unable to locate the footpath. As the conditions worsened, it became apparent that the trio would not be able to get out, or back to Camp Muir that night. Realizing the gravity of the situation, Michael put up his tarp and made the best arrangements possible to keep them warm and provide water. The group spent two nights under this tarp and in Michael's care while waiting for a break in the weather. The break came on Tuesday morning. With a break in the fog and clouds, Michael was able to ascertain their position, which allowed the trio to promptly descend.

It's important to note that Michael's skill, preparedness, and personal effort probably saved the lives of Delorenzo and Lance. This incident highlights the fact that even the most experienced mountaineers can get caught off guard in a seemingly benign situation. There is nothing very technical about descending the Muir Snowfield, yet incidents here are relatively frequent. In low visibility, knowing your position and direction of travel will make a significant difference in the remainder of your day.

Using a compass, map, altimeter, and GPS may have gotten them back on route in a short period of time. Without these tools, it's hard to discern up from down in a whiteout. Exposure on the Muir Snowfield can easily make a person hypothermic in a very short period of time: part of the reason that the Muir Snowfield claims more lives than any place on Mount Rainier. The importance of staying together as a group is also highlighted—especially when gear and tools are divided among group members.

An additional factor in this case is that incorrect information on trip plans led to the delay in rescue efforts for Delorenzo and Lance. (Source: Mike Gauthier, Climbing Ranger)

(Editor's Note: When guiding on Mount Rainier in the early 60's, I kept a piece of paper with the compass bearing from Camp Muir to Paradise in my pocket. On my third guided climb, I needed it to negotiate a whiteout from Camp Muir while descending with three clients.

It is good to see so few incidents from Mount Rainier again this year. Readers are reminded to check out www.mountrainierclimbing.blogspot.com for up to date information.)

FALL ON ICE, CLIMBING GEAR IN PACKS—CLIMBING UNROPED
Washington, Alpine Lakes Wilderness Area, Sherpa Peak
On September 25, Otto Vaclavek (53) died of hypothermia after falling between 100 and 150 feet down an ice slope and over a cliff. Vaclavek had no broken bones, so it's unclear why he didn't move from the location where rescue crews found him.

His son Max Vaclavek (12) died of head injuries suffered in the fall, even though he was wearing a helmet.

Investigators believe both father and son fell at the same time. They were not using climbing ropes or harnesses, just ice axes and crampons.

Sharon Marion, wife of Otto and mother of Max, said her husband was very familiar with the area.

Rescuers found backpacks. They were hidden underneath rocks. Deputies say it's not uncommon for hikers to leave heavy gear behind, but they usually come back to retrieve it. The backpacks contained their tent, sleeping bags, and some climbing gear. (Source: From a report found at KREM.com)

Analysis

This is an unfortunate case, especially as it involves a father and son. Both were avid outdoor enthusiasts. Otto Vaclavek came to the U.S. in 1988, having been granted political asylum from Czechoslovakia. While Sherpa Peak is a technically difficult climb with complex terrain, it is believed that the two had the skill levels to accomplish the route. The mystery is why their climbing gear was in their packs. (Source: Jed Williamson)

(Editor's Note: In terms of other Washington climbing areas that normally see at least a few accidents each year, Kelly Bush, Wilderness District Ranger for North Cascades National Park, reported that there were no mountaineering accidents there in 2007. There were several hikers rescued, including two fatalities, however.)

FALL ON ROCK, INADEQUATE PROTECTION, CARABINER CAME OFF SLING, EXCEEDING ABILITIES
West Virginia, New River Gorge National Park, Beauty Mountain

On August 19, approximately twelve or fifteen feet up on a route called "Brainteasers" (5.10 a), CU (21) placed a medium-sized hex, which was attached to the rope via a standard length sling. About eight to ten feet higher, CU placed a medium sized nut in a thin vertical crack. It too was attached to the rope via a standard length sling. CU struggled about six to seven feet higher and placed a 0.75 cam in an upward flaring vertical crack. No more than one foot above this placement, CU became fatigued and casually yelled, "Falling," to his belayer, RE (24). RE took in slack expecting to catch a small fall. Instead, CU fell approximately 30 feet and hit the ground, landing on his back.

CU was totally unresponsive for several minutes upon landing and appeared to be in extreme pain. Fearing the worst, RE called 911 and an intensive rescue took place. CU was evacuated from the cliff by stretcher and then airlifted to a hospital in Charleston, WV. He suffered a broken right scapula, several broken ribs, and a bruised lung. He was released from the hospital the next day.

Analysis

All three placements had failed. The upper piece, the 0.75 cam, was poorly placed (as the crack flared upward). The impact of the fall deformed the cam. An examination of the damage to the cam after the fall showed that the downward lobes of the cam were actually *over*-cammed and the upper lobes were *under*-cammed. Because the upper lobes were not contracted, it is clear that the cam rotated out of the crack.

The second placement, the nut, was well placed and never left the crack during the fall. However, the lower carabiner that was attached to the sling (the same sling that was attached to the nut) somehow became disengaged from the rope and thus never caught the fall. The sling remained attached to the nut in the rock after the fall, although it was missing the bottom carabiner, which would normally have been attached to the rope.

An examination of the nut after the fall showed that it had never been fully weighted, as there were no scars or abrasions on it. (The nut was new and painted). Furthermore, the carabiners that attached the nut to the sling and the sling to the rope were wire-gate 'biners with very stiff gates. Hence, "gate-flutter" was very unlikely. There were also no obvious corners or protrusions in the wall that could have forced the carabiner gate open to make it pop off of the sling. The sling was probably caught in the carabiner gate at the time of the fall and subsequently popped out of the 'biner once the sling was weighted, causing the rope to become totally disengaged from the sling. This was entirely possible due to the fact the sling was a skinny "dyneema" type.

The first piece of protection, the hex, was poorly placed. It was capable of holding only one-directional force. It popped completely out of the rock during the fall, most likely when the belayer, RE, took in slack.

This route was probably a poor choice for CU. Earlier that day, he had some difficulty top-roping a climb of the same grade. CU had never trad-climbed a route harder than a 5.7 in his life. Furthermore, it had been more than a year since he had last led a climb using traditional protection. His experience with traditional climbing was limited. He has led fewer than 20 traditionally-protected pitches total since he first began climbing. As a result, CU struggled to place (and clip) reliable protection while on the climb.

Additionally, he climbed very little over the past year, so lacked the physical stamina necessary to complete such a climb. RE's instincts told him that the idea of CU leading Brainteaser was a disaster waiting to happen. RE relayed these thoughts to CU many times before starting the climb.

Nevertheless, CU should not have hit the ground from this fall. His second placement was totally "bomber." Neither he nor his belayer noticed that the sling was caught in the lower carabiner as he climbed (assuming that this was actually what happened). It was a stroke of bad luck that the lower carabiner became disengaged from the sling, as this seems to be a rare occurrence.

Although it would not have caught his fall even if it had held, his first piece of protection, a hex, was not a good choice. The first piece of protection should always be multi-directional. Had he placed a cam instead of a hex, which was possible, the first piece may have never popped out of the rock.

It is interesting to note that out of eleven people total at the cliff that day, no one had a cellphone! It took more than ten minutes running back to the cars to call for help. If possible, climbers should always bring a cellphone to this crag. It is also important for climbers to know exactly where they are and how to get there, as rescue personnel may not be wholly familiar with the area.

Additional Comment: CU was fortunate that he was young and in excellent physical condition. His back was unusually muscular and may have safeguarded him from more serious injury. CU has since recovered from his injuries and has returned to climbing. (Source: Edited from a report by Rick Evans)

FALL ON ROCK, INADEQUATE PROTECTION
West Virginia, New River Gorge, Endless Wall

On November 12, rangers and Fayette County Emergency Services personnel rescued a climber (age unknown) who had fallen at the Endless Wall climbing area. Rangers Randy Fisher and Karl Keach, working with only a general description of the location of the accident, received through a 911 call, searched for and found the caller, who led them to the scene. Keach coordinated the rescue from the top of the cliff while Fisher employed a series of ladders and ropes to reach the injured climber, who had suffered numerous fractures and lacerations. An 80-foot litter raise was conducted to bring him to the top of the cliff. He was then wheeled out on a litter and flown to the Charleston area trauma center.

Analysis

An investigation revealed that the climber had removed his gear from the second bolt and was attempting to down-climb when he fell about 20 feet as he tried to traverse from the route he was on to another route called "Nasty Groove."

This was the fourth time a climber has fallen this year—a significant increase in climbing-related incidents. The causes included bad belays, traditional gear pulling from the rock, and poor climbing decisions. New River Gorge is a world-class climbing destination, with 1600 traditional and sport routes. It has miles of high-quality sandstone cliffs with an extraordinary diversity of climbing routes. (Source: From reports submitted by Gary Hartley, Chief Ranger, and Aram Attarian)

(Editor's Note: While Ranger Hartley indicates that the number of incidents represents a "significant increase," it would seem to be a low number given the

popularity of this climbing area. Estimates of climbers visiting here each year run from several hundred to over a thousand.)

FALL ON SNOW/ICE FROM ANCHOR POINT—APPARENT ANCHOR FAILURE DUE TO EXTERNAL FORCES
Wyoming, Grand Teton National Park, Grand Teton

On April 29, Alan Rooney (38) and Jonathan Morrow (28) fell to their deaths while attempting an alpine climb on the northwest side of the Grand Teton. They fell about 1,500 feet down a very steep couloir containing several prominent ledges. Rooney and Morrow had accessed that side of the Grand Teton from the Lower Saddle via the Valhalla Traverse prior to attempting to climb either the Enclosure Couloir or the Black Ice Couloir.

A significant Search and Rescue (SAR) operation ensued, involving National Park rangers, US Forest Service heli-tack crewmembers, and a helicopter. A team of three rangers climbed to an area close to the Enclosure Couloir from which they were able to observe the two men 1,500 feet below.

Analysis

After rangers in the helicopter were able to confirm that both climbers had apparently fallen to their deaths, the ground team shifted their focus to getting back to the Lower Saddle and switching to the recovery phase of the operation. Consequently, we did not go to what we surmise was the accident scene located about 100 meters and out of sight to our east. A more thorough investigation of the accident scene was therefore not conducted. We can only make suppositions based upon evidence found much lower with the fallen climbers, conditions as we observed them, past weather, and institutional knowledge concerning events of the past that have occurred in the same area. Additionally, knowledge gained by the conduct of mountain climbing patrols in this area was particularly useful.

• Alan Rooney and Jonathan Morrow were avid climbers, mountaineers, and skiers. The area they had decided to climb was well within their ability level. They were both highly competent, driven mountaineers and well within their comfort level while climbing across the Valhalla Traverse.

• It is known from eyewitness accounts that they got started nearly two-and-a-half hours later than they wanted from their bivouac site. The Lower Saddle would have been a more desirable starting location. Additionally, from the times registered on the photographs, they were moving slowly as they made their way from the Meadows to the Saddle, and then across the Valhalla Traverse. The Valhalla Traverse contained large sections of unconsolidated powder snow on breakable crust. Conditions like these would likely have led to exhausting and time-consuming post holing.

• The temperatures at the 10,450-foot level for the period of April 28th to the 29th were above freezing. Their plan to climb on the north side of the

Grand Teton may have been influenced by the fact that most of the area remains in the shade.

• Typically, for alpine climbing in this area, climbers want cold conditions. With overnight low temperatures well below freezing, objective hazards such as rock, snow, and ice are frozen in place, and present less of a threat to the alpine climber. Even with cold overnight low temperatures, as the day warms up, rocks will loosen and snow will have more of a tendency to slide or slough off. In this case temperatures were not below freezing and a significant warm-up was occurring.

• The tracks observed from the helicopter place the two men in the very bottom of the Enclosure Couloir. From the time registered on the last photograph, this was nearly noon on the 28th. Because they were found clipped to the same sling with locking carabiners, one can presume that they were both at the same stance. From the other photographs we know that they were belaying and placing and removing protection as they climbed across the Valhalla Traverse. Therefore, whatever befell the two climbers, it happened while they were at a stance, or belay position.

• Because of their experience we can assume that they had constructed what they considered to be an adequate anchor at this stance, because they had both connected themselves securely to it. The nature of the anchor is not known, however, because the rescue team did not go to that location. The sling that they were clipped into could have been placed over a projecting rock in the couloir, over an ice ax or axes jammed into the snow slope, or may have been a part of a more extensive anchor.

• For the anchor to have failed, it must have been acted upon by some external force. The force could have been an avalanche, rockfall, a snow slough that was substantial enough to knock the climbers off of their stance, or a combination of these external forces. With the ambient air temperatures as high as they were that day, an avalanche or slough is likely. In fact, avalanches were observed by others on the north facing side of some of the peaks in the south fork of Garnet Canyon that day.

In conclusion, the tracks seen by rangers Springer and Guerierri put the two men in the Enclosure Couloir. The time on the final photograph was at noon. Both men were at a belay stance clipped in to the same anchor. The precise nature of the anchor is not known. The anchor was acted upon by some external force that resulted in the failure of the anchor and the subsequent fall suffered by the two climbers. The weather, specifically the warm air temperatures, most likely played a key role in the incident. Regrettably, weather and snow conditions combined with human factors resulted in the tragic death of two much-loved and respected members of the local climbing community. (Source: Chris Harder, Investigating Ranger)

FALLING ROCK—HANDHOLD PULLED OFF, FALL ON ROCK, HASTE, NO HARD HAT
Wyoming, Grand Teton National Park, Base of Irene's Arête

June 24. Leading on 5.3 terrain. Fifty feet of rope out. Number 3 Camalot at my knee. Trying to go fast. Pulled on a hold. It broke off. I tipped over backwards. Bounced and fell 30+ feet on rock fins and ledges. Rope came taught right as I hit a large ledge. Camalot did not pull out.

Analysis
Should not have fallen even when hold broke. Helmet would have eliminated 12 of my 45 stitches. Could have been worse! (Source: Phil Powers, 46)

FALL ON ROCK, INADEQUATE EQUIPMENT
Wyoming, Grand Teton National Park, Mount Moran

On July 28th, Alison Arnold (53) fell approximately ten to 15 feet while descending the CMC route on Mount Moran. Arnold was down-climbing into the Drizzlepuss Notch near the bottom of the CMC route as she slipped and fell. While falling, Arnold struck her face on a rock, then landed on her feet, causing damage to her face and ankles. Arnold's partners helped her ascend to the top of the Drizzlepuss Notch, then down the East Face of The Drizzlepuss to a location where they spent the night.

Early on the morning of July 29th the Arnold party was encountered by another climbing party that had a cellular phone and was able to contact NPS Dispatch. A subsequent rescue was conducted utilizing a helicopter short-haul insertion of rescue personnel and extraction of the patient.

Analysis
Alison stated that she has been climbing in and around the Teton Range for about 40-plus years. Alison's footwear consisted of hiking shoes with non-sticky rubber soles. She was not wearing a helmet and was down-climbing unroped. After a successful ascent of Mount Moran on the CMC route, she was descending near the bottom of the CMC route into the Drizzlepuss Notch. About 6:30 p.m., her feet slipped, and as she fell, her head struck the rock and her feet hit a small ledge that flipped her onto her back.

She was wearing a small backpack along with a climbing rope coiled across her back. The fall caused her to land flat on her backpack and rope, saving her from possible serious injury. (Source: Chris Harder, Ranger and Incident Commander)

FALLING ROCK—THROWN FROM RIDGE
Wyoming, Wind River Range, Leg lake Cirque

On August 11, Luke Rodolph (23) stood on the rim of Upper Silas Canyon with three of his friends. He allegedly looked over the edge of the rim and didn't see anyone. He then threw a rock about the size of a basketball off and looked over again to "...watch it fall, see where it was going to hit..."

The rock struck longtime NOLS instructor Pete Absolon (47) in the head and killed him instantly.

As of the date of publication, no charges have been filed against Mr. Rodolph. The Attorney for Fremont County, Ed Newell, said that Rodolph would not be charged for several factors, including the following: Rodolph immediately took responsibility for his actions, was extremely remorseful, didn't intend to cause harm, had no criminal history, and served in Iraq. (Source: From an article in *The Star-Tribune*, by Joshua Wilson)

Analysis

Falling rocks and objects are an inherent risk for climbers. As I stated in an editorial for the 1995 issue of ANAM, "A mountain hazard that is present for everyone from drivers on switchback roads to the most avid wall climbers is falling rocks. They can be unloosed by the forces of nature—geology, weather, and gravity..." or dislodged by people. Further, "Upon occasion, dislodging rocks is done purposely. To 'clean' the top or part of often used routes is commonplace, with care being taken to ensure that the landing zone is clear."

Falling rocks (and other objects such as ice and full water bottles) are the third leading cause of serious injuries and fatalities, mostly because of direct hits to the skull.

The most common human factors that come in to play are 1) not wearing a climbing helmet and 2) being in a poor position—i.e., directly under loose rock or another climbing party—or, as in this case, random individuals who may be on the ridge or summit above. The latter factor suggests the range of possibilities that humans are capable of engaging in.

The experienced climbing community knows that it is possible to dislodge rocks accidentally, either with feet or hands. That is why great care is taken not to do so, even if no individual or party is apparently below. Those who are new or novice climbers, including clients with guides, are most often the ones who make this error.

When rocks or objects (such as ice, carabiners, water bottles, etc) are dislodged, it is common etiquette and the accepted practice to shout, "ROCK!" That word is universally understood to mean that something is falling. Such terms as, "Watch out!" or "Oh, no!" can be confusing.

What climbers do not expect is for people to be deliberately throwing rocks or objects from above or "trundling" (pushing on large rocks with both feet to dislodge them), even in remote areas. These days, there is a likelihood that even in deep wilderness there may be climbers or others below.

In September of 1994, three young men from Bozeman trundled rocks from Granite Peak (12,799 feet) that resulted in a cascade of an estimated 50 tons dropping 1,000 feet, killing climber Tony Rich. The young men were charged with negligent endangerment. Their sentences included fines and expenses for rescue/recovery and for family counseling, community service.

In the mountains, the rules of the game for all constituents include care to avoid accidentally triggering rockfall. It is never acceptable to deliberately dislodge or throw rocks.

Meanwhile, Pete Absolon's widow, Molly, the family, NOLS staff and friends, and the Lander community will continue to grieve and try to make sense out of this seemingly senseless event. (Source: Jed Williamson)

FALL ON ROCK, INADEQUATE PROTECTION AT RAPPEL ANCHOR
Wyoming, Grand Teton National Park, Grand Teton

At approximately 1500 on August 15, Teton Interagency Dispatch Center (TIDC) received a cellphone call from Matej Bosak. Mr. Bosak reported that his uncle, Vladimir Wojnar (55), fell while descending the west side of the Grand Teton. He stated they were near the Upper Saddle and his uncle had lost consciousness and was bleeding from a head wound. I was notified of this incident shortly after 1500. I requested all available Jenny Lake Rangers report to the Rescue Cache and that one of the Teton Interagency Contract Helicopters be staged at Lupine Meadows.

About 1530, I spoke with Mr. Bosak via telephone. He stated that his uncle was conscious but didn't remember falling. He expressed concern about the bleeding from his uncle's head wound and wasn't sure if they could safely descend.

About 1600, Ranger Andy Byerly arrived at the Lower Saddle. He had hiked to the Lower Saddle during a scheduled patrol. Bill Liberatore, a guide for Exum Mountain Guides, offered to help with the rescue. At 1615, Byerly and Liberatore left the Lower Saddle and started climbing toward the accident site. While they were climbing, Rangers Motter and Bywater flew near the west side of the Grand Teton. They confirmed that Bosak and Wojnar were near the bottom of Sergeant's Chimney, which is a few hundred feet below the summit. After a thorough reconnaissance of the accident site, Motter, Bywater and the helicopter pilot Jon Bourke decided that a short haul extraction from the base of Sergeant's Chimney was possible. Motter and Bywater were dropped off at the Lower Saddle. They started to climb to the accident site at approximately 1645. Two shuttle flights from Lupine Meadows brought four additional rangers and rescue gear to the Lower Saddle where they staged during the rescue.

Byerly and Liberatore arrived at Sergeant's Chimney at 1715. Motter and Bywater arrived at 1800. At 1730, Byerly reported that Wojnar had fallen approximately 15 feet and had sustained a head injury, head wound, and a laceration on his right elbow. Wojnar had lost conscious for approximately one minute and had no recollection of the event. Dr. Will Smith listened to Byerly's full report of the patient's condition. A group decision was made to move Wojnar approximately 60 feet down to a ledge where he would be extracted via short haul.

After a thorough reconnaissance check flight of the extraction site, a group decision was reached that a short-haul operation was appropriate and a litter and additional medical equipment was short hauled to the site at 1830. The patient was packaged and extracted from the site at 1915. He was flown without a litter attendant to the Lower Saddle.

With the patient at the Lower Saddle, the helicopter returned to Lupine Meadows, where it was changed from a short-haul to an ambulance configuration. It returned to the Lower Saddle where Wojnar was placed into the helicopter and flown to Lupine Meadows. He was transferred to an ambulance, which departed for St John's Hospital at 2015.

Analysis

I interviewed Matej Bosak during the evening of August 15 at the Rescue Cache at Lupine Meadows. He stated that he and his uncle, Vladimir Wojnar, had camped at the Meadows in Garnet Canyon the night of August 14. They departed the Meadows at 0700 on August 15. Without incident, they climbed the Grand Teton via the Owen Spaulding route. They reached the summit at 1430. During the descent they decided to rappel Sergeant's Chimney. They only had one Figure-8 descending device, which they planned to share. Bosak rappelled the chimney without incident. He attached the Figure-8 to the end of the rope and Wojnar began pulling up the rope. Bosak heard a noise, looked up and saw Wojnar sliding down the rope only using gloved hands. Bosak then saw him let go of the rope and fall approximately 15 feet.

I later interviewed Vladimir Wojnar, who was at St. John's Hospital at the time. He wasn't quite sure what happened, but he seemed to recollect slipping while pulling up the rope with the attached Figure-8. He believes he grabbed the rope when he fell and doesn't remember anything after that. He wasn't wearing a helmet and wasn't attached to the rappel anchor. Wojnar stated that he had climbed the Grand Teton six times.

Perhaps if Mr. Wojnar had been securely attached to the rappel anchor he may not have fallen while pulling the rope with attached Figure-8. Perhaps wearing a helmet may have prevented his head injury. (Source: Ron Johnson, Ranger and Incident Commander)

FALLING ROCK—DISLODGED BY CLIMBER, OFF ROUTE, BENIGHTED, EXCEEDING ABILITIES

Wyoming, Grand Teton National Park, Mount Owen

On August 29 at 1300, I received a report via park dispatch that a climbing party on Serendipity Arête (Mount Owen) reported (via cellphone) hearing calls for help from the area of the North Ridge of the Grand Teton. The park contract helicopter and available rescue personnel were dispatched to the Lupine Meadows Rescue Cache. The subsequent recon flight of the area located a climbing party adjacent to the Third Ice Field in the area of the Black Ice Couloir. Initially the party was observed to be moving and did not obviously indicate a need for assistance. No other parties were observed in the search area. An additional flight, confirmed via a message board used in the helicopter, that the above party was indeed in need of a rescue and that one of the party members, Robert Campbell (65), was injured. Ranger Visnovske was inserted via shorthaul to the rescue site from a landing zone in Valhalla Canyon at 1901. Visnovske assessed the climbers and found that Campbell had a severe injury to his right hand and various bruises sustained in a leader fall. Visnovske determined that a shorthaul extraction via screamer suit of both climbers was warranted. Visnovske and the two climbers were then extracted in a single load and delivered to the Valhalla Canyon landing zone. The climbers were flown internally, accompanied by Ranger Byerly, to Lupine Meadows. Campbell was transported to St. John's Hospital by ambulance.

At the Rescue Cache, the climbers told me that they had left the Lower Saddle at 0700 on Tuesday with the intent to climb the North Ridge of the Grand Teton via the Valhalla Traverse. They got off route and while climbing in an area of very loose rock, Campbell pulled out a large, loose block that struck his legs and severely injured his right hand. The party attempted to climb to a suitable bivouac ledge, but was benighted at a confined and uncomfortable belay. On Wednesday morning, they attempted to ascend, but were unable to do so because of Campbell's injuries. They then decided to traverse and then descend to a larger ledge below them. They heard voices and began to yell for help. They felt that their cries for help were understood, which was confirmed later by the arrival of the helicopter. Though their need for help was not initially apparent to rescuers, fortunately it was confirmed, and they were rescued.

Analysis

In a debriefing with Campbell and his partner Ullmann, they told me that they met at the AAC Climbers' Ranch in the park and decided to climb the North Ridge of the Grand Teton. They camped Monday night on the Lower Saddle and left for the Valhalla Traverse at about 0700 on Tuesday morning. They came around the Valhalla Traverse and descended the ramp, but "somehow missed the first ledge." From their description and location, they likely traversed higher than they should have to reach the Grandstand, instead ascending to the left of the Black Ice Couloir toward the west face. The area where they were climbing is known to be very loose with poor quality rock. Sometime in the evening while Campbell was leading, he pulled on the large boulder that released. Ullmann climbed to him and they tried to bandage his hand and stop the bleeding. Ullmann then tried to lead a pitch to a ledge where they could spend the night. Campbell, unable to use his hand, could not climb and at some point hung in the rope for about 30 minutes unable to move. Ullmann rappelled to him in an effort to assist. Ultimately, they rappelled some distance farther and spent the night in a confined and uncomfortable bivouac location.

In the morning, they tried to ascend with Ullmann leading. Campbell was still unable to follow. Then Campbell led a traversing pitch because he felt that he could see the Grandstand. They heard voices and began to yell for help. Hoping that help would come, they began descending to a large ledge. When the helicopter came into view, they told me that they waved. When the helicopter came close, Ullmann told me she was pointing to a ledge below her where she expected to meet the helicopter. When I asked her if she thought a helicopter could land there, (it could not), she said that she didn't know if it could land, but thought that a person might be able to get out. She did say that she told Campbell he needed to look more in need of assistance when the helicopter was in view. Ultimately the helicopter returned, and they were able to communicate their need for assistance.

Campbell and Ullmann were off route. Without prior knowledge of the route, crossing the Valhalla Traverse and climbing to the North Ridge requires significant route finding. Many parties find themselves off route in this area. Once Campbell was injured, they attempted to provide appropriate first aid and to affect their own rescue. Movement was difficult, and not knowing where they were, they were forced to bivouac. Campbell was the more experienced mountaineer, and Ullmann a self-described 5.7 leader. (Source: Scott Guenther, Ranger and Incident Commander)

FALL ON ROCK—DISLOCATED SHOULDER
Wyoming, Grand Teton National Park, Symmetry Spire

At 1330 on September 11, the Exum Mountain Guides' office received a call from Guide Gary Falk, guide, on Jensen ridge of Symmetry Spire. Falk stated that a client had a dislocated shoulder and a helicopter would be needed at the base of Jensen Ridge at 1430. SAR coordinator Jim Springer was contacted by phone. In a later call Falk stated that the accident occurred at 1130 on the second pitch of the route. The subject had taken a short pendulum fall, belayed from above, and while trying to hold himself, dislocated his shoulder. Falk lowered the subject and a second client to the base of the climb.

At 1430, contract helicopter 20HX flew to the scene from the Lupine Meadows Rescue Cache for recon. Helicopter 20HX inserted Ranger Chris Harder via short-haul to the base of the route at 1502. The patient was packaged, placed in a screamer suit, and, with Harder attending, was short-hauled from the scene to the Lupine Meadows Rescue Cache at 1600. The patient was then transported to St. Johns Hospital in park ambulance.

Analysis

While being belayed from his guide above, Kliger was climbing a section of 5.7 rock when he fell. In an attempt to maintain his stance, Kliger held onto the rock with one hand and subsequently dislocated his shoulder. (Source: Jim Springer, Ranger and Incident Commander)

(Editor's Note: This accident was one of eight this year in which the climber dislocated a shoulder.

Also of note from Wyoming is that there were two backcountry fatalities that were the result of avalanches. One involved two brothers skiing in Darby Canyon, Pete Maniaci (20's), who survived, and Paul Maniaci (also 20's), who could not be resuscitated after his brother freed him. He had been buried four feet.

There were no details available for the other fatality, which occurred south of Jackson.)

STATISTICAL TABLES

TABLE I
REPORTED MOUNTAINEERING ACCIDENTS

	Number of Accidents Reported		Total Persons Involved		Injured		Fatalities	
	USA	CAN	USA	CAN	USA	CAN	USA	CAN
1951	15		22		11		3	
1952	31		35		17		13	
1953	24		27		12		12	
1954	31		41		31		8	
1955	34		39		28		6	
1956	46		72		54		13	
1957	45		53		28		18	
1958	32		39		23		11	
1959	42	2	56	2	31	0	19	2
1960	47	4	64	12	37	8	19	4
1961	49	9	61	14	45	10	14	4
1962	71	1	90	1	64	0	19	1
1963	68	11	79	12	47	10	19	2
1964	53	11	65	16	44	10	14	3
1965	72	0	90	0	59	0	21	0
1966	67	7	80	9	52	6	16	3
1967	74	10	110	14	63	7	33	5
1968	70	13	87	19	43	12	27	5
1969	94	11	125	17	66	9	29	2
1970	129	11	174	11	88	5	15	5
1971	110	17	138	29	76	11	31	7
1972	141	29	184	42	98	17	49	13
1973	108	6	131	6	85	4	36	2
1974	96	7	177	50	75	1	26	5
1975	78	7	158	22	66	8	19	2
1976	137	16	303	31	210	9	53	6
1977	121	30	277	49	106	21	32	11
1978	118	17	221	19	85	6	42	10
1979	100	36	137	54	83	17	40	19
1980	191	29	295	85	124	26	33	8
1981	97	43	223	119	80	39	39	6
1982	140	48	305	126	120	43	24	14
1983	187	29	442	76	169	26	37	7
1984	182	26	459	63	174	15	26	6
1985	195	27	403	62	190	22	17	3
1986	203	31	406	80	182	25	37	14

	Number of Accidents Reported		Total Persons Involved		Injured		Fatalities	
	USA	CAN	USA	CAN	USA	CAN	USA	CAN
1987	192	25	377	79	140	23	32	9
1988	156	18	288	44	155	18	24	4
1989	141	18	272	36	124	11	17	9
1990	136	25	245	50	125	24	24	4
1991	169	20	302	66	147	11	18	6
1992	175	17	351	45	144	11	43	6
1993	132	27	274	50	121	17	21	1
1994	158	25	335	58	131	25	27	5
1995	168	24	353	50	134	18	37	7
1996	139	28	261	59	100	16	31	6
1997	158	35	323	87	148	24	31	13
1998	138	24	281	55	138	18	20	1
1999	123	29	248	69	91	20	17	10
2000	150	23	301	36	121	23	24	7
2001	150	22	276	47	138	14	16	2
2002	139	27	295	29	105	23	34	6
2003	118	29	231	32	105	22	18	6
2004	160	35	311	30	140	16	35	14
2005	111	19	176	41	85	14	34	7
2006	109		227		89		21	
2007	113		211		95		15	
Totals	6,333	958	11,536	2003	5,342	715	1,409	292

TABLE II

Geographical Districts	1951–2006			2007		
	Number of Accidents	Deaths	Total Persons Involved	Number of Accidents	Deaths	Total Persons Involved
CANADA*						
Alberta	520	142	1033			
British Columbia	317	119	641			
Yukon Territory	37	28	77			
New Brunswick	1	0	0			
Ontario	37	9	67			
Quebec	31	10	63			
East Arctic	8	2	21			
West Arctic	2	2	2			
Practice Cliffs[1]	20	2	36			
UNITED STATES						
Alaska	499	183	844	14	5	26
Arizona, Nevada Texas	90	18	160	3	0	10
Atlantic–North	956	147	1646	21	1	34
Atlantic–South	98	25	169	9	0	17
California	1265	294	2517	21	1	36
Central	134	17	217	1	0	1
Colorado	755	212	2288	12	1	20
Montana, Idaho South Dakota	79	32	126	4	0	8
Oregon	200	110	454	7	1	17
Utah, New Mexico	162	58	299	5	1	10
Washington	1036	317	16	7	2	15
Wyoming	553	128	997	9	3	17

*No reports from 2006–2007

[1]This category includes bouldering, artificial climbing walls, buildings, and so forth. These are also added to the count of each province, but not to the total count, though that error has been made in previous years. The Practice Cliffs category has been removed from the U.S. data.

TABLE III

	1951–06 USA	1959–04 CAN.	2007 USA	2007 CAN.
Terrain				
Rock	4378	528	75	
Snow	2304	355	32	
Ice	259	158	7	
River	14	3	0	
Unknown	22	10	0	
Ascent or Descent				
Ascent	2926	587	68	
Descent	2227	371	46	
Unknown	249	13	0	
Other[N.B.]	7	0	0	
Immediate Cause				
Fall or slip on rock	3467	290	55	
Slip on snow or ice	990	207	20	
Falling rock, ice, or object	614	137	9	
Exceeding abilities	540	32	7	
Illness[1]	382	26	11	
Stranded	335	53	4	
Avalanche	286	127	3	
Rappel Failure/Error[2]	284	47	7	
Exposure	270	14	2	
Loss of control/glissade	206	17	1	
Nut/chock pulled out	206	9	14	
Failure to follow route	179	30	7	
Fall into crevasse/moat	159	50	4	
Faulty use of crampons	102	6	5	
Piton/ice screw pulled out	95	13	0	
Ascending too fast	65	0	1	
Skiing[3]	55	11	1	
Lightning	46	7	0	
Equipment failure	15	3	0	
Other[4]	438	37	28	
Unknown	61	10	0	
Contributory Causes				
Climbing unroped	1004	165	3	
Exceeding abilities	895	202	10	
Placed no/inadequate protection	714	96	22	
Inadequate equipment/clothing	672	70	11	
Weather	467	67	4	
Climbing alone	394	69	3	
No hard hat	337	71	6	

	1951–06 USA	1959–04 CAN	2007 USA	2007 CAN
Contributory Causes (continued)				
Inadequate belay	202	28	7	
Nut/chock pulled out	199	32	1	
Poor position	168	20	9	
Darkness	141	21	5	
Party separated	117	12	2	
Failure to test holds	100	32	1	
Piton/ice screw pulled out	86	13	0	
Failed to follow directions	73	12	0	
Exposure	64	16	0	
Illness[1]	40	9	0	
Equipment failure	11	7	0	
Other[4]	260	100	4	
Age of Individuals				
Under 15	1243	12	2	
15-20	1266	203	5	
21-25	1388	257	19	
26-30	1273	211	15	
31-35	1063	114	17	
36-50	1207	143	30	
Over 50	226	31	21	
Unknown	1959	530	18	
Experience Level				
None/Little	1759	304	9	
Moderate (1 to 3 years)	1595	354	24	
Experienced	1902	440	72	
Unknown	2025	559	20	
Month of Year				
January	224	25	5	
February	206	55	4	
March	303	68	4	
April	401	39	6	
May	900	62	18	
June	1044	70	16	
July	1121	254	13	
August	1027	184	19	
September	1165	75	14	
October	448	42	6	
November	188	20	6	
December	97	24	3	
Unknown	17	1	0	
Type of Injury/Illness (Data since 1984)				
Fracture	1219	223	40	

	1951–06 USA	1959–04 CAN	2007 USA	2007 CAN
Type of Injury/Illness (Data since 1984) (Continued)				
Laceration	685	71	18	
Abrasion	330	76	9	
Bruise	462	83	15	
Sprain/strain	331	33	19	
Concussion	225	28	10	
Hypothermia	154	16	2	
Frostbite	125	12	0	
Dislocation	117	16	8	
Puncture	44	13	1	
Acute Mountain Sickness	43	0	1	
HAPE	71	0	1	
HACE	25	0	0	
Other[5]	315	49	8	
None	225	188	14	

N.B. Some accidents happen when climbers are at the top or bottom of a route, not climbing. They may be setting up a belay or rappel or are just not anchored when they fall. (This category created in 2001. The category unknown is primarily because of solo climbers.)

[1]These illnesses/injuries, which led directly or indirectly to the accident, include fatigue (3), snow blindness (2), hypothermia, dislocated shoulder reaching for a hold (2), and AMS.

[2]These include rappelled off the end of the rope, uneven ropes, mistook 5m mark for middle of rope, attached climbing rope to gear loop on harness, and lowering errors (5).

[3]This category was set up originally for ski mountaineering. Backcountry touring or snowshoeing incidents—even if one gets avalanched—are not in the data.

[4]These include failure to disclose medical Hx to guide (2), failed to wear eye protection (2), overconfidence, became ill because he was "psyched by the big wall", jumped into a crevasse while wearing crampons, injured while doing a pendulum, ice ax on pack instead of in hand (3), unable to self-arrest, climber fell because he dislodged a rock, lost (on descent from Camp Muir), failure to follow instincts, inadequate supervision, poor communication, and rock thrown from ridge deliberately.

[5]These included snow blindness (2); seizures; atrial fibrillation; tension pneumothorax (2); bruised lung; early stage exhaustion, fatigue and hypothermia; teeth knocked out, severed artery, vein, and ligament; crushed his fingers when he dislodged a rock.

(Editor's Note: Under the category "other," many of the particular items will have been recorded under a general category. For example, the climber who dislodges a rock that falls on another climber would be coded as Falling Rock/Object. A climber who has a hand or foot-hold come loose and falls would be coded as Fall On Rock and Other – and most often includes Failure To Test Holds.)

MOUNTAIN RESCUE UNITS IN NORTH AMERICA
**Denotes team fully certified—Technical Rock,
Snow & Ice, Wilderness Search;
S, R, SI = certified partially in Search, Rock, and/or Snow & Ice

ALASKA
Alaska Mountain Rescue Group. PO Box 241102, Anchorage,
AK 99524. www.amrg.org
Denali National Park SAR. PO Box 588, Talkeetna, AK 99676.
Dena_talkeetna@nps.gov
US Army Alaskan Warfare Training Center. #2900 501 Second St., APO AP 96508

ARIZONA
Apache Rescue Team. PO Box 100, St. Johns, AZ 85936
Arizona Department Of Public Safety Air Rescue. Phoenix, Flagstaff, Tucson,
Kingman, AZ
Arizona Division Of Emergency Services. Phoenix, AZ
Grand Canyon National Park Rescue Team. PO Box 129, Grand Canyon, AZ 86023
****Central Arizona Mountain Rescue Team/Maricopa County Sheriff's Office
MR.** PO Box 4004 Phoenix, AZ 85030. www.mcsomr.org
Sedona Fire District Special Operations Rescue Team. 2860 Southwest Dr.,
Sedona, AZ 86336. ropes@sedona.net
****Southern Arizona Rescue Assn**/Pima County Sheriff's Office. PO Box 12892,
Tucson, AZ 85732. http://hambox.theriver.com/sarci/sara01.html

CALIFORNIA
****Altadena Mountain Rescue Team.** 780 E. Altadena Dr., Altadena, CA 91001
www.altadenasheriffs.org/rescue/amrt.html
****Bay Area Mountain Rescue Team.** PO Box 19184, Stanford, CA 94309 bamru@
hooked.net
California Office of Emergency Services. 2800 Meadowview Rd., Sacramento, CA.
95832. warning.center@oes.ca.gov
****China Lake Mountain Rescue Group.** PO Box 2037, Ridgecrest, CA 93556
www.clmrg.org
****Inyo County Sheriff's Posse SAR.** PO Box 982, Bishop, CA 93514 inyocosar@
juno.com
Joshua Tree National Park SAR. 74485 National Monument Drive,
Twenty Nine Palms, CA 92277. patrick_suddath@nps.gov
****Los Padres SAR Team.** PO Box 6602, Santa Barbara, CA 93160-6602
****Malibu Mountain Rescue Team.** PO Box 222, Malibu, CA 90265.
www.mmrt.org
****Montrose SAR Team.** PO Box 404, Montrose, CA 91021
****Riverside Mountain Rescue Unit.** PO Box 5444, Riverside,
CA 92517. www.rmru.org   rmru@bigfoot.com
San Bernardino County Sheriff's Cave Rescue Team. 655 E. Third St.
San Bernardino, CA 92415
www.sbsd-vfu.org/units/SAR/SAR203/sar203_1.htm
****San Bernardino County So/ West Valley SAR.** 13843 Peyton Dr., Chino Hills, CA
91709.

San Diego Mountain Rescue Team. PO Box 81602, San Diego,
CA 92138. www.sdmrt.org

San Dimas Mountain Rescue Team. PO Box 35, San Dimas, CA 91773

Santa Clarita Valley SAR / L.A.S.O. 23740 Magic Mountain Parkway,
Valencia, CA 91355. http://members.tripod.com/scvrescue/

Sequoia-Kings Canyon National Park Rescue Team. Three Rivers, CA 93271

Sierra Madre SAR. PO Box 24, Sierra Madre, CA 91025.
www.mra.org/smsrt.html

Ventura County SAR. 2101 E. Olson Rd, Thousand Oaks, CA 91362
www.vcsar.org

Yosemite National Park Rescue Team. PO Box 577-SAR,
Yosemite National Park, CA 95389

COLORADO

Alpine Rescue Team. PO Box 934, Evergreen, CO 80437
www.alpinerescueteam.org

Colorado Ground SAR. 2391 Ash St, Denver, CO 80222
www.coloradowingcap.org/CGSART/Default.htm

Crested Butte SAR. PO Box 485, Crested Butte, CO 81224

Douglas County Search And Rescue. PO Box 1102, Castle Rock, CO 80104.
www.dcsarco.org info@dcsarco.org

El Paso County SAR. 3950 Interpark Dr, Colorado Springs,
CO 80907-9028. www.epcsar.org

Eldorado Canyon State Park. PO Box B, Eldorado Springs, CO 80025

Grand County SAR. Box 172, Winter Park, CO 80482

Larimer County SAR. 1303 N. Shields St., Fort Collins, CO 80524. www.fortnet.
org/LCSAR/ lcsar@co.larimer.co.us

Mountain Rescue Aspen. 630 W. Main St, Aspen, CO 81611
www.mountainrescueaspen.org

Park County SAR, CO. PO Box 721, Fairplay, CO 80440

Rocky Mountain National Park Rescue Team. Estes Park, CO 80517

Rocky Mountain Rescue Group. PO Box Y, Boulder, CO 80306
www.colorado.edu/StudentGroups/rmrg/ rmrg@colorado.edu

Routt County SAR. PO Box 772837, Steamboat Springs, CO 80477
RCSAR@co.routt.co.us

Summit County Rescue Group. PO Box 1794, Breckenridge, CO 80424

Vail Mountain Rescue Group. PO Box 1597, Vail, CO 81658
http://sites.netscape.net/vailmra/homepage vmrg@vail.net

Western State College Mountain Rescue Team. Western State College Union,
Gunnison, CO 81231. org_mrt@western.edu

IDAHO

Bonneville County SAR. 605 N. Capital Ave, Idaho Falls, ID 83402
www.srv.net/~jrcase/bcsar.html

Idaho Mountain SAR. PO Box 741, Boise, ID 83701. www.imsaru.org
rsksearch@aol.com

MAINE

Acadia National Park SAR. Bar Harbor, Maine

MARYLAND
**Maryland Sar Group. 5434 Vantage Point Road, Columbia, MD 21044
Peter_McCabe@Ed.gov

MONTANA
Glacier National Park SAR. PO Box 128, Glacier National Park,
West Glacier, MT 59936
Flathead County Search and Rescue. 920 South Main St., Kalispell, MT 59901.
Sheriff's Office phone: 406-758-5585.

NEVADA
**Las Vegas Metro PD SAR. 4810 Las Vegas Blvd., South Las Vegas,
NV 89119. www.lvmpdsar.com

NEW MEXICO
**Albuquerque Mountain Rescue Council. PO Box 53396, Albuquerque,
NM 87153. www.abq.com/amrc/ albrescu@swcp.com

NEW HAMPSHIRE
Appalachian Mountain Club. Pinkham Notch Camp, Gorham, NH 03581
Mountain Rescue Service. PO Box 494, North Conway, NH 03860

NEW YORK
76 SAR. 243 Old Quarry Rd., Feura Bush, NY 12067
Mohonk Preserve Rangers. PO Box 715, New Paltz, NY 12561
NY State Forest Rangers. 50 Wolf Rd., Room 440C, Albany, NY 12233

OREGON
**Corvallis Mountain Rescue Unit. PO Box 116, Corvallis, OR 97339
www.cmrv.peak.org
(S, R) **Deschutes County SAR.** 63333 West Highway 20, Bend, OR 97701
**Eugene Mountain Rescue. PO Box 20, Eugene, OR 97440
**Hood River Crag Rats Rescue Team. 2880 Thomsen Rd., Hood River,
OR 97031
**Portland Mountain Rescue. PO Box 5391, Portland, OR 97228
www.pmru.org info@pmru.org

PENNSYLVANNIA
**Allegheny Mountain Rescue Group. c/o Mercy Hospital,
1400 Locust, Pittsburgh, PA 15219. www.asrc.net/amrg
**Wilderness Emergency Strike Team. 11 North Duke Street, Lancaster,
PA 17602. www.west610.org

UTAH
**Davis County Sheriff's SAR. PO Box 800, Farmington, UT 84025
www.dcsar.org
Rocky Mountain Rescue Dogs. 3353 S. Main #122, Salt Lake City, UT 84115
**Salt Lake County Sheriff's SAR. 3510 South 700 West, Salt Lake City, UT 84119
San Juan County Emergency Services. PO Box 9, Monticello, UT 84539

**Utah County Sherrif's SAR. PO Box 330, Provo, UT 84603. ucsar@utah.uswest.net

**Weber County Sheriff's Mountain Rescue. 745 Nancy Dr, Ogden, UT 84403. http://planet.weber.edu/mru

Zion National Park SAR. Springdale, UT 84767

VERMONT
**Stowe Mountain Rescue. P.O. Box 291, Stowe, VT 05672 www.stowevt.org/htt/

VIRGINIA
Air Force Rescue Coordination Center. Suite 101, 205 Dodd Building, Langley AFB, VA 23665. www2.acc.af.mil/afrcc/airforce.rescue@usa.net

WASHINGTON STATE
**Bellingham Mountain Rescue Council. PO Box 292, Bellingham, WA 98225

**Central Washington Mountain Rescue Council. PO Box 2663, Yakima, WA 98907. www.nwinfo.net/~cwmr/ cwmr@nwinfo.net

**Everett Mountain Rescue Unit, Inc. 5506 Old Machias Road, Snohomish, WA 98290-5574. emrui@aol.com

Mount Rainier National Park Rescue Team. Longmire, WA 98397

North Cascades National Park Rescue Team. 728 Ranger Station Rd, Marblemount, WA 98267

**Olympic Mountain Rescue. PO Box 4244, Bremerton, WA 98312 www.olympicmountainrescue.org information@olympicmountainrescue.org

Olympic National Park Rescue Team. 600 Park Ave, Port Angeles, WA 98362

**Seattle Mountain Rescue. PO Box 67, Seattle, WA 98111 www.eskimo.com/~pc22/SMR/smr.html

**Skagit Mountain Rescue. PO Box 2, Mt. Vernon, WA 98273

**Tacoma Mountain Rescue. PO Box 696, Tacoma, WA 98401 www.tmru.org

North Country Volcano Rescue Team. 404 S. Parcel Ave, Yacolt, WA 98675 www.northcountryems.org/vrt/index.html

WASHINGTON, DC
National Park Service, EMS/SAR Division. Washington, DC

US Park Police Aviation. Washington, DC

WYOMING
Grand Teton National Park Rescue Team. PO Box 67, Moose, WY 83012

Park County SAR, WY. Park County SO, 1131 11th, Cody, WY 82412

CANADA
North Shore Rescue Team. 147 E. 14th St, North Vancouver, B.C., Canada V7L 2N4

**Rocky Mountain House SAR. Box 1888, Rocky Mountain House, Alberta, Canada T0M 1T0

MOUNTAIN RESCUE ASSOCIATION
PO Box 880868
San Diego, CA 92168-0868
www.mra.org • www.mountainrescuehonorguard.org

Fran Sharp, President
Tacoma Mountain Rescue Unit, WA
president@mra.org
253-691-3773 (phone)   360-482-6187 (fax)
Term expires June 2008

Charley Shimanski, Vice President
Alpine Rescue Team, CO
vp@mra.org
303-832-5710 (work)   303-674-7937 (home)
303-909-9348 (cell)
Term expires June 2008

Dan Land, Secretary/Treasurer/CFO
San Dimas Mountain Rescue Team
sectreas@mra.org
909-268-2237 (cell)   909-621-9988 (home)

Glenn Henderson, Member at Large
Riverside Mountain Rescue, CA
glennrobin@hotmail.com
951-925-4848 (home)   951-317-5635 (cell)
Term expires 2008

Mike Vorachek, Member at Large
Bonneville County SAR
mtnsar@cableone.net
208-553-5724 (work)   208-521-6882 (cell)

Kayley Trujillo, Executive Secretary/Treasurer
978 Camino de la Reina #34
San Diego, CA 92108
info@mra.org
858-229-4295 (phone)   619-374-7072 (fax)
(Appointed position)